D0362450

The Teaching Assistant's Gui.
Emotional and Behavioural Difficulties

Also available from Continuum

The Teaching Assistant's Guide to Emotional and Behavioural Difficulties

Kate Spohrer

continuum

Continuum International Publishing Group

The Tower Building   80 Maiden Lane
11 York Road   Suite 704
London, SE1 7NX   New York, NY 10038

www.continuumbooks.com

British Library Cataloguing-in-Publication Data
A catalogue record for this book is available from the British Library.

ISBN: 9-780-8264-9838-0 (paperback)

Illustrations by Kate Spohrer
Typeset by Kenneth Burnley, Wirral, Cheshire
Printed and bound in Great Britain by MPG Books Ltd, Bodmin, Cornwall

Contents

Introduction

Acknowledgements

Thanks go to all of the families I have worked with and learned so much from. Thanks also to my mother, son and partner. Without their inspiration, patience and support this book would not have been possible. Thanks also to Tividale Community Arts College nurture group staff and children, and to Christine Cooke.

Setting the scene

When I was asked to write this book I had some reservations. Fundamentally I resist any labels that talk in terms of difficulty or deficit. I prefer to think of emotional health and well-being than emotional and behavioural difficulties. However we live in a world that seems to like to focus on the negative, despite psychologists telling us that we cannot conceptualize the negative. After a good stern talk to myself, I decided to rise to the challenge of writing this book. My influences as you will see are eclectic. I dismiss no theory completely, but also embrace none to the exclusion of all others.

How to use this book

This book is written with a view to it being scanned from cover to cover, with more time being taken on the areas that are of particular interest and relevance to the reader. My recommendation would be to ensure completion of the activities and the quizzes which appear at the end of all but the final chapter. In the appendix the quizzes appear along with possible answers and additional comments.

What is EBD?

Why you need to know about emotional and behavioural difficulties

You may have come across this little story before. It is freely available on the internet and is anonymous so I can attribute it to no one. It is a very thought provoking story which I hope you will take time to read before you go on because it explains why we need to understand emotional and behavioural difficulties (EBD) far better than I could. You can find a version at www.toddlertime.com/advocacy/pat/person-feelings.htm

The very small person who had feelings

Once there was a very small person who had feelings. They had many feelings and felt them every day. Their family liked it when they showed their feelings. So they started wearing them on their sleeve. One day one of the parents said they did not like to see the small person's FEAR feeling anymore, so the small person tried to pull it off. The parent said they would give the small person some TOUGH to cover FEAR. It was very hard to cover the FEAR with TOUGH so the other parent and the grandparents helped. This took many days. 'Now you look wonderful,' the parents said when it was done. 'We've covered some of your feelings with TOUGH. You will grow into a good strong person.'

When the small person was a little older they found a friend. The friend also wore their feelings on their sleeve. One day the friend said, 'My parents want me to cover up my LONELY feeling and I will be different from now on.' And the friend was! The small person decided to cover LONELY feelings too and got ANGER from another adult. The small person put the patches of ANGER on top of their LONELY. It was hard work trying to cover the LONELY feelings.

One day when the small person went to school some of their LONELY feelings started to show. So, the teacher kept them after school and gave them some GUILT to cover the LONELY feelings. Sometimes at night when they were alone the small person would look at all their feelings. They would pull off TOUGH and ANGER to look at LONELY and FEAR. Then it would take a long time to put the TOUGH, ANGER and GUILT on again.

One night the small person noticed their LONELY and FEAR were growing and beginning to stick out around the patches. The small person believed that they had to go out to find some more ANGER to cover the LONELY and to get all the TOUGH that their parents could spare to cover FEAR.

This small person grew bigger and was very popular. Everyone said that this person could hide their feelings well. One day the person's parents said they had a PROUD feeling because the person had so much TOUGH. But the person could not find anywhere to put the PROUD feeling because the TOUGH was getting so big. The small person had trouble finding any room on their sleeve for any other feelings, TOUGH and the ANGER were all that showed.

Then one day the small person met another person and they became friends. They thought that they were a lot alike because they both had only TOUGH and ANGRY feelings showing. But one day the friend told the small person a secret. 'I'm not really like you. . . my TOUGH and ANGRY are really only patches to hide my FEAR and LONELY.' The friend then pulled back the edge of their TOUGH and showed the person FEAR. Just for a second.

The small person sat quiet and did not speak. Then carefully they pulled back a little edge of TOUGH and showed their FEAR. The friend could also see the LONELY underneath. Then the friend gently reached out and touched the small person's FEAR and then the LONELY. . . The friends touch was like magic. A feeling of ACCEPTANCE appeared on the small person's sleeves, and the TOUGH and ANGER were smaller. Then the small person knew that whenever someone gave them ACCEPTANCE they would need less TOUGH and there would be more room to show their REAL feelings whatever they were . . . HAPPY . . . LONELY . . . PROUD . . . SAD . . . LOVING . . . STRONG . . . GOOD . . . WARM . . . HURT . . . FEAR . . . .

Meet the virtual EBD class

Let me introduce you to our virtual group. The pupils in the group are of mixed ages. Read through and see if any of the children have similarities to children you work with. Even if the children are of ages you do not currently work with, it is a good idea to read through the case studies as this could be the child you work with in the future, or in the past, and it all helps to increase understanding of this complex group of children. At the end of each case study is a sentence or two explaining how the child makes the teacher feel. This is of crucial importance – to notice how the child makes you feel, because as illustrated so well in the story above, human beings transfer feelings from one to another. If you want to understand someone else, observe how they make you feel, that is often how they are feeling.

Ryan, Fabio, Pete, Mia, Joe, Deano, Hayley, Joanna, John, Amina, Ahmed

Ryan

Ryan is in reception. Ryan finds integrating with the other children difficult and to begin with his main method of communication was to go and hit somebody. This inevitably caused complaints from parents. Ryan is of mixed race parents, and lives with his father. He never sees his mother, who lives in another country. His dad is out at work a lot, but does do his best to spend as much time as possible with Ryan, however much of Ryan's time is spent with carers. Sometimes he is left at school at the end of the day for rather a long time. At these times he becomes withdrawn and anxious. Mondays are days when he is particularly disruptive in school. His teachers work very hard to include him fully in lessons and he gets plenty of opportunity to shine, but this is draining for the teachers in the classroom. Sometimes it feels like Ryan just isn't understanding what is going on around him, he seems to be in his own world, and at times will make rude signs to children or trot out the odd swear word and exhibit a very slight facial tic. Ryan's teacher is very aware of how problems in reception can develop into serious EBD issues if they are not handled sensitively at this stage. As a consequence she has queried Tourette's with the educational psychologist and has been advised to try to substitute the unwanted behaviour with something that is all right to do. She is now working on replacing the rude sign with a thumbs up. However, because of his outbursts to other children and the complaints made by other parents, the school is becoming increasingly concerned that they will have to exclude him. They have tried using 'time out' as a measure to give him time to calm down, and to communicate to him that some of his behaviour is not acceptable.

Ryan's teacher says being with Ryan makes her feel frustrated, useless, anxious, scared and isolated, 'as if she is speaking a different language' – just not understood.

Fabio

Fabio is in Year 2. Fabio shouts out a lot in class, is very fidgety and frequently uses inappropriate sexualized language. He has recently moved to his sixth school. He will leave the classroom without permission, sometimes leaving the school premises and putting himself at risk. He lives with his mother, who was very young when she had him, close to his maternal grandmother and her boyfriend who seem to have a lot to do with his care. He has an uncle who is the same age as himself. Fabio is struggling with his work at school. He seems constantly distracted and unable to focus on his work, wishing instead to move his position, sit under a table or against a wall, even getting into a cupboard on one occasion. His teacher, an NQT tries to engage regularly with his mum, who frequently does not attend meetings. She is quite perplexed and upset by his behaviour, but she is receiving regular supervision from the behaviour advisory teacher which she says helps her to understand his emotional state and as a consequence helps her to cope with the pressure she feels he puts her under in the class.

Fabio's teacher reports she feels exhausted, frustrated, angry, and anxious when with Fabio. She does however hold on to the desire to succeed with him. She sees her job with children like Fabio a little bit like climbing a mountain – you have to learn to work with the mountain to get to know it, because if you don't, it will beat you.

Amina

Amina is in Year 3. On the outside Amina can appear quiet, shy and withdrawn. On the inside she would love to express herself but somehow just can't summon up the confidence to do so. She will go into class and sit at the back keeping away from the action. She is likely to be ignored by people because she looks stand-offish and aloof. She tends to make few friends, and prefers them to be from outside school. She appears to find it difficult to interact with her peers. She interacts better with adults or children of a different age to herself. Academically she never seems to excel, finding it difficult to pay attention to detail, but always does well enough to get by. Her teachers tend to leave her alone most of the time. When put under any pressure she refuses to speak for a while. Amina suffers from high frequency hearing loss, but has not been able to find a hearing aid to help. She works hard to get by contextually. Recently Amina has been developing a reluctance to attend school. Her mum reports she has never liked school, but now she really seems to hate it.

Amina's teachers say she causes them little trouble, but if anything they feel 'distant' from her.

Hayley

Hayley is in Year 4. She is in long-term foster care, but would like to go back to live with her mother. Sadly this is unlikely to happen, but Hayley believes she will go back to mum and is living in constant hope. Hayley was put at risk when at home, and it is possible she was sexually abused by one of her mum's boyfriends.

Hayley has been in this school for a few months and has made a friend. Hayley's literacy and numeracy skills are poor. She finds following a logical argument perplexing. Her teachers report that sometimes she does not seem to understand what you are talking about because her answers are so unrelated to the question. Hayley has been known to take things that aren't hers from home and school. She also tells lots of fibs, seemingly believing they are true. This dishonesty bothers her teacher a lot. Hayley seems to drift in school. She can spend a whole lesson having achieved very little. She likes to just chat with her friend. A recent faecal smearing episode in the toilets was thought to be Hayley's work. Despite all of this Hayley gets on well with her class teacher who tries hard to love Hayley.

Hayley's teacher reports Hayley makes her feel despondent, lost, confused, and isolated. Hayley's teacher gets regular support from the behaviour advisory teacher who runs a group which she attends once a month for 'supervision' purposes. This gives her a chance to talk about problems she is facing in a constructive way, and use the rest of the group to help her contain all the emotions that are whizzing around the classroom. She says, 'If it weren't for this group I'd have had a breakdown and be out of teaching by now.'

Pete

Pete is in Year 5. Pete has seven siblings, three younger and four older. He is a boy who at times it was difficult to rationalize with. He is often bragging about the number of fights he has been in at the weekend. His relationship with his father is difficult as his dad has been detained at Her Majesty's pleasure. Staff report that he does seem to hold his dad in high esteem, even though he has not seen him for a long time. Pete is poor academically.

Language rules were hard for him to understand and his maths is very rudimentary too. He is not a boy to pick an argument with, and has been known to overturn tables in the classroom when enraged – quite a frightening sight for his classmates, with much heavy breathing and a genuine sense of being out of control. To get the best out of him his teacher always tries to stay several steps ahead making sure he is faced with situations he is able to deal with. Although not a problem every lesson, he poses a sinister threat in the classroom. What seems to work best are very clear boundaries so he feels safe, but ensuring he has some choice and feeling of control within those safe boundaries. However, he can still 'kick off' without warning which is what makes him so hard to teach. His teacher is convinced that although she has not been able to tune in to the warning signs thus far, there must be some which if she looks hard for she will find. Consequently she has been practising developing enhanced sensory acuity to tune in and calibrate better on his behaviour. This helps her to feel more in control of the room.

Pete's teacher reports at times feeling scared, confused, vulnerable, penetrated, 'living on a knife edge'.

Deano

Deano is in Year 6. He has attended 10 schools so far as his family never seem to stay in one place for very long. His reading skills are poor. His numeracy is a little better. Attendance is an issue; he is frequently not in school on a Friday. He scares his teachers and other pupils because of his outright defiance. Fights in the playground are common. He seems to be involved in 'family feuds' on a regular basis. Friendships are hard for him to make and keep, he prefers to stick with his extended family for support. His teacher says she feels threatened when with him, and that she needs to be constantly vigilant because she can never be sure what he is going to do next, 'some minutes you think you have some communication with him, the next minute it is almost as if he doesn't know who you are'. Deano will often rip up his work if there is a tiny mistake on it, which there usually is; he seems to find it really hard to take a risk. He is a very hard boy to like.

Deano's teacher reports that he makes her feel anxious, threatened, 'like being on a knife edge' when he is in the class-room. Secretly she prefers it when he is away from school and can feel a sigh of relief ripple through her body, and a feeling of togetherness with the rest of the class when she does the register and he is not there. This makes her feel guilty. There is some-thing of an outsider feeling about Deano.

Joe

Joe is in Year 7. He lives with his father and has not seen his mother for a very long time. He, his father and his sister moved to the area a few months ago from about 50 miles away. He has an older family from a previous relationship of his dad's and an older full sister. He is a bright lively boy, looks angelic, but signifi-cantly underachieves in his academic work. Joe was excluded from his previous school for violent behaviour towards a member of staff. He often appears not to be listening to his teachers, preferring to talk, pull faces, pinch, shove or kick his fellow class-mates – this causes them some annoyance – but he can always tell you what the teacher has been saying. He has been known to get into scuffles with other children, not only in the playground, but also in the classroom. He will happily engage in arguments and swearing with girls and boys in his class. He is given to leaving school without permission. Some of his teachers are very patient with him, especially the female ones, but he tends to get on less well with male teachers. Even the teachers he gets on well with at times have more trouble than they feel they can cope with. He is a real challenge in the classroom but is also a child who 'gets under your skin' emotionally.

Joe has spent four mornings a week in the school's nurture group where he is able to operate at a developmentally appropriate level. Staff in the nurture group report that he has become far more settled and contained whilst with them over the year. He is now able to make attachments to staff and his behaviour is improving in lessons too.

His teachers report that he can make them feel powerless, frustrated, confused, infuriated, angry and isolated, but that he also has the ability to make them feel a great sense of achievement when they have had a good lesson with him.

Ahmed

Ahmed is in Year 8. Ahmed has had difficulties in school and at home for a long time. In primary school he disrupted the class by shouting out, swearing, going off task and engaging in conversation with other pupils when he and they should have been working. In the playground he was very boisterous and got drawn into silly behaviour like throwing stones at teachers' cars. In nursery school he smacked a teacher's bottom. At home his mother reports he has always been very lively, needing lots of her attention. When he was small she felt she could never go out for a meal or to a friend's house because he would crawl all over her, or be rushing round breaking stuff.

He showed a lot of talent in the dramatic arts. He also enjoys art and science. To begin with he settled into the high school quite well, but the staff gradually became exasperated with his behaviour which was becoming more and more disruptive. Ahmed has never been malicious. He is described as charming and a boy you just can't fail to see the nice side of, but in the classroom he is a real trial. He is of average to above average ability, but is underperforming in school. Ahmed is at risk of permanent exclusion for his persistently disruptive behaviour. Ahmed is often to be found out of the lesson. Ahmed's mum is supportive of the school, but also feels privately that the school are not accepting Ahmed for the person he is.

Ahmed's teachers feel very exasperated and frustrated by Ahmed because they think he has ability, but will not achieve potential because he doesn't concentrate on his work.

Joanna

Joanna is in Year 9. She is very overweight. She has been to the doctor for advice on her diet, but finds sticking to it very difficult. She rarely attends school and has fallen way behind in her studies. She lives with her mother and father, both of whom are registered disabled. She finds getting school clothes to fit difficult, which further puts her off going into school. Joanna seems to have little enthusiasm for life. Because she is rarely in school she has no good relationships with adults at the school. The closest she has to this is her relationship with the school's education welfare officer who has worked hard at building a relationship with Joanna and her parents. Joanna finds taking risks difficult and doesn't seem to want to take the chance of failing on anything. Any work she does which isn't what she considers perfect she will destroy.

Joanna's teachers report they feel sapped of energy when they have been with Joanna for a while. 'It feels like you are giving, giving, giving with Joanna, and nothing seems to come back. She is just immoveable. I find her really hard to keep going back to, I just want to shake her up and get some life into her.'

Mia

Mia in Year 10, likes to give the boys the run around and is believed to be sexually active. She gives her mum hell, says she wants to leave home as soon as she gets to 16 and there is nothing she can do to stop her. Mia has been known to climb out of windows to escape from home. At school she gets into trouble for talking, rudeness to teachers, telling fibs and leaving the premises without permission. Mum reports that, as a young child, she was into everything, restless and found sleeping difficult, and has always been a bit precocious as regards the opposite sex. It is possible to have a really adult discussion with this young lady, who in many ways appears very mature. She finds making friends of her own age quite easy, but keeping them difficult. Friendships tend to be superficial and run into trouble oscillating between good mates with a group of girls, then being really into her boyfriend of the moment. She is academically able, but likely to seriously underperform due to behavioural difficulties. Her teachers worry about this underperformance and she says they 'are always on at me that I should do better, and I get pissed off with them telling me that, they don't know what it's like to be inside my head, and if they are so keen on me doing well why do they keep tipping me out of lessons?' She seems to operate best when in an adult world and given responsibility. Due to her father's job the family have moved from one end of the country to the other, so Mia has had to change schools several times.

Mia's form tutor reports feeling at times elated then just as quickly deflated by Mia's behaviour, also, frustrated, amused, fascinated, sad and anxious. At times she feels she can resonate with Mia because she reminds her of herself at 15. Some of Mia's other teachers don't get on as well with her.

John

John is in Year 11 and very close to permanent exclusion for violent and abusive behaviour in school. He lives with his mother and stepfather, seeing his father every month or so, when he turns up. He seems to have no concept of remorse or conscience. He frightens his teachers and seems to rule some of his classmates, acquiring 'friends' through fear. He will look you straight in the eye and swear black is white. He is quite a bright boy who could gather a number of GCSEs. His aspirations are to become a bricklayer, but he seems to show no real practical inclination towards achieving this. The words 'menacing, frightening, threatening, sinister, sly, clever' have all been attributed to this boy. His parents are at their wits' end with him and feel they have no communication with him. At home he goes out and comes in when he pleases. He is 'beyond control'. He has already been involved with the police for antisocial behaviour out on the streets. He hangs out with a bunch of older lads who are well known to the police for drug associated crime. John does not have any good relationships with adults in the school. Everyone seems to feel worn out by John.

John's teachers report that when they are with him they feel anxious and have a heightened sense of danger; 'it's a bit electrifying being with John, but not in a positive sense. You feel like you are going to get the shock, not like he is going to help you by using it against the common enemy'.

The case studies above, from our virtual school, are provided to help you identify with the kind of young people this book is about.

Activity: Visualize an EBD child

Sit quietly with your eyes closed for a moment and visualize a child you know that you believe to have EBD characteristics, like those children above. Also note how the child makes you feel when you are in their company. Then open your eyes and quickly jot down as many of their characteristics and feelings as possible. Look at your writing and if you haven't written 5 feelings close your eyes again and go back into the room with the child. See what you saw, smell what you smelled, hear what you heard, feel what you felt, and write down the feelings. Looking at how people make us feel can often help us understand how they are feeling – that puts us in a much better position to be able to help them.

To be successful with a child with EBD you need an understanding of what it is like to be a child with EBD. You also need some understanding of your own make-up and response to the child. Some people have a natural ability to empathize with EBD children and can get the best out of them – others have to learn how.

Emotional and behavioural difficulties – a definition

The term Emotional and Behavioural Difficulties is a catch all, muddy, and not totally useful term. It encompasses difficult to cope with behaviour exhibited by children for a huge number of reasons. Autism, Asperger's, ADHD, Attachment Disorders, Fragile X syndrome, Tourette's, etc. can all from time to time fall into the cornucopia of EBD. Attempts have been made at defining EBD, and it is possibly fair to say that it is the educational world's answer to the multifarious labels attributed to children by the medical world. It could be seen as an attempt at taking some of the medicalization and labelling out of the equation, and adding some emotional understanding in. In practice what EBD means is that a child fails to thrive educationally, socially and emotionally. The external manifestation of this failure is likely to be severe acting out or acting in behaviour, both of which are a serious cause for concern for the adults around the child, and a communication from the child that all is not well in their world. EBD happens when emotional health and well-being are out of balance.

The revised SEN Code of Practice (DfES 2001b) Section 7:60 provides a definition of EBD thus:

> Children and young people who demonstrate features of emotional and behavioural difficulties, who are withdrawn or isolated, disruptive and disturbing, hyperactive and lack concentration; those with immature social skills; and those presenting challenging behaviours arising from other complex special needs.

It goes on to suggest extra help or counselling may be required for:

- flexible teaching arrangements
- help with development of social competence and emotional maturity
- help in adjusting to school expectations and routines
- help in acquiring the skills of positive interactions with peers and adults
- specialized behavioural and cognitive approaches
- re-channelling or refocusing to diminish repetitive and self-injurious behaviours
- provision of class and school systems which control and censure negative or difficult behaviours and encourage positive behaviour
- provision of a safe and supportive environment.

With this definition in mind, I propose to examine some of the theories surrounding behaviour, and suggest some useful strategies that you can use on a day to day basis in your work in the classroom.

Understanding EBD through different theories on behaviour

Below is an appetite-whetting tour of some of the psychological perspectives on behaviour. It is not meant to be detailed as this book is more practically based; however, if you want to read more have a look at *Perspectives on Behaviour* (2000) and *Psychology for Teaching Assistants* (2005) (see References).

Humanistic

First I want to introduce you, or reintroduce you if you have already met, to a man who to my mind makes great sense when trying to help us understand the behaviour of people around us. That man is Abraham Maslow.

Abraham Maslow was of the **humanistic** school of psychology and in 1954 he proposed we are all motivated by needs and that our needs are arranged in a hierarchy. At the bottom of the hierarchy are basic physical needs, for example food, water, warmth, shelter, air, sleep. The next level is that of safety and security, health and family. Up a further level he placed love and belonging, friendships and family. It is around this level that we are expecting children to operate in school. On the next level came self esteem, confidence, achievement, respect for others and respect by others. At the very top is self-actualization where a sense of morality, creativity, spontaneity, problem solving, lack of prejudice and acceptance of facts is gained.

Maslow's Hierarchy of Needs theory (1954) states that we must satisfy each need in turn and only when the lower-order needs of physical and emotional well-being are satisfied are we concerned with the higher-order needs of influence and personal development. If the lower-order needs are not met, we are no longer concerned about the maintenance of our higher-order needs. Consequently when we want children to operate at levels three and four of the hierarchy we need to make sure needs at levels one and two are met. The needs requirement differs from child to child and we must understand the needs of the child if we are to be able to meet them.

Humanistic psychology tries to maximize a person's potential by minimizing those things that get in the way of progress. It focuses on setting up to succeed rather than setting up to fail.

Behaviouristic

The **behaviourist** is concerned with a person's outward expression of behaviour. The behaviour is believed to be the result of a person's learning and not due to cognitive or unconscious processes. Behaviourism is very scientific in its approach to understanding how unwanted behaviour can be changed. The most famous behaviourist is Pavlov who conducted experiments with dogs and bells, eventually training the dogs to salivate at the sound of a bell, because he had sounded a bell each time the dog was exposed to food, hence the eventual link in the dog's brain between bell and salivation. Clearly if the dog were to be able to understand the manipulation, and be able to override the conditioning he would no longer salivate at the sound of a bell. We all get conditioned in ways that affect our behaviour and sometimes it only takes a very brief experience to set up a reaction, particularly if the experience is a traumatic one.

Behaviourism is really all about 'training' and 'getting things into the muscle'. It focuses totally on observable behaviour and does not concern itself with what is going on inside a person to create that outward expression. Behaviourism is believed to be useful for retraining where unacceptable behaviour has taken root, but it does not address psychodynamic unconscious processes or cognitive issues. For this reason it is most useful if taken hand in hand with other theories.

A behavioural psychologist will look at what people do, rather than what they say, or what they say they do. Behaviourists have looked at the learning of less complex animals than the human animal, like Pavlov and dogs, Skinner with rats and pigeons. These psychologists observed that rewarding the behaviour you want to see more of results in a type of conditioning that meant the behaviour was more likely to be repeated. This sounds very simple and like common sense, but in practice it often backfires, because human beings starved of adequate and appropriate attention (which can be required in very different amounts by different people depending on the individual's attention need) will substitute the gratification by receiving attention for doing good things, by attention for doing negative things (because that is the only attention they seem to get). They will then keep repeating the negative behaviour because it gets their attention needs met. This is why behaviour feedback for the good things a child does needs to be frequent and specific, and to out number the negative feedback in a ratio of 4:1.

We can learn a lot about training our children from the way we train our dogs. This might sound initially like dreadful child abuse, but think for a minute, we cannot rely on complex language with animals; we have to rely on very clear feedback. We treat a dog when it has done what we want it to do, we lavish praise, and we don't expect the dog to be able to guess what we are thinking. We give a dog clear yes and no signals and we create clear boundaries. We are rewarded by well behaved animals that are capable of saving our lives. Maybe there is something to learn here. What do you think?

Cognitive

The cognitive-behavioural approach developed because the behavioural approach observed that people respond to stimuli in different ways, so it was thought that thinking may be having an impact on the responses people were giving. If this was the case, it could be possible to change thinking to change behaviour. Cognitive behavioural therapy (CBT) is very popular at the moment. CBT relies heavily on rationalization and focuses on how you think about yourself, the world and other people and how what you do affects your thoughts and feelings. Changing the way you think can help you to feel better. Unlike psychoanalysis and some of the other talking based therapies, it focuses on the 'here and now' problems and difficulties. Instead of focusing on the causes of your distress or symptoms in the past, it looks for ways to improve your state of mind now. Neuro-Linguistic Programming (NLP) has similarities with cognitive as well as psychodynamic theories because it uses the unconscious mind to affect the thinking; however, NLP works really fast, believing that the mind needs to change patterns of operating really quickly to be effective. There will be much more on using NLP later in the book.

Psychodynamic

Some children seem to defy good practice and still disrupt even the best run classroom. They do not respond well to positive teaching, they seem to deskill and demoralize their teachers. They are very challenging. If we believe that behaviour is communication and therefore has some kind of meaning we can set to work to try to learn the language of the child and understand what it is they are saying. The problem is that each child seems to have their own unique dialect, so it takes some time to calibrate on this behaviour. Understanding the meaning enables the teacher to step away from the negative feelings engendered by a pupil's defensive behaviour patterns. The relationship the teacher has with the child is crucial to success in the classroom. The psychodynamic perspective on behaviour believes the origin of behaviour difficulties stems from the unconscious mind. There are both unconscious and conscious processes going on in our mind at any one time. We are driven by primitive programmes and we are often not consciously aware of these and what they are striving for. Our conscious mind will try to make sense of things and avoid anxiety, but in the process it may engage in a number of things the psychoanalysts call projection, displacement, sublimation, transference, splitting, denial, introjection and rationalization. These behaviours can be very difficult to understand, particularly if you are the person who catches the 'fallout'. This fallout has, according to psychoanalytic theory, been set up many years before in the early care giving relationships. To understand what is going on in behaviour today the psychoanalyst will look back to childhood. Psychoanalytic theory has had many advocates as well as many opponents. It is complex and time consuming, but there are some very useful aspects that can be used in schools to better understand ourselves and the young people we work with, with very positive outcomes. Attachment theory, which is discussed below, was borne out of psychodynamic thinking. Attachment theory is the basis for the Nurture Groups now growing in popularity in the UK. Attachment theory is discussed more fully in Chapter 2 of this book. Another extremely useful device, also discussed later in this book, which has come from the psychodynamic stable, is that of 'reflective teams' or 'work discussion groups', which offer a type of group supervision to people working in the emotionally charged climate of the classroom.

Some teachers have a great ability to make children feel valued, safe, contained, and to meet their needs so that they can learn. These teachers show the pupils that they hold them in mind when they are not there. (I remember a time when I baked a cake and brought it in for an anger management group I was running. The children were completely different that week with the knowledge, which at first they could not believe, that I had actually baked a cake for them, that I had thought about them when I was away from them, and that those thoughts had been positive enough to drive me to bake a cake. They seemed so much calmer and more willing to please, it was remarkable. (I would probably have to have my kitchen inspected by environmental health and go on a food hygiene course to do this now!) Others seem to rub children up the wrong way; they create a hostile culture in their rooms and don't seem to like their pupils very much. They almost appear to persecute them. On the other hand a teacher who values pupils conveys a real liking and respect for their pupils. Most teachers will be somewhere between the two most of the time. In your role as TA, you will have been in a privileged position to see these different styles of teaching, and you will unconsciously and maybe consciously have reflected on the teaching styles, and maybe even considered which style you use when you are working with children. Strange as it may seem, you have probably seen more teachers teach than the teachers you see teach have. You have a great basis on which to build your practice.

Social learning theory

Social learning theory grew out of the behaviourist school and was popularized by Albert Bandura, who was very interested in the concept of modelling. We often talk of 'role models' people with whom we identify and whose actions we wish to emulate. Bandura however was mainly concerned with the emergence of aggression in children following exposure to violence either on TV or in real life. His work has been widely influential in criminology. Social learning theory looks at the way we can be introduced to behaviours that we see, but have never crossed our minds before, and then begin to engage in them. We will also look at them and assess whether or not to try them, and with an incomplete picture make a decision that its probably OK because nothing has happened to 'so and so' who did 'such and such'. However the reality sometime later could be very different. . . when we have time to reflect from our prison cell.

Social learning theory, though, has something to offer on a positive note. We can use modelling for positive effects and the system of Neuro-Linguistic Programming does just that.

Social learning theory denies the biological influence in a person's behaviour.

Ecosystemic

The ecosystemic theory is based on systems theory and family therapy where the behaviour is made sense of in terms of the system within which it operates. All parts of the system will affect all other parts, so what happens in one bit may be reflected in other parts or may have positive or negative effects on other parts. The ecosystemic model always reminds me of one of those balloons with bits sticking out – squeezing one bit causes a change somewhere else.

Family therapy employs the ecosystemic approach, and it is worth considering the school as a family. In a family, behaviour patterns are often repeated even when they have negative outcomes, because the equilibrium will be maintained, and this in its own way is more comfortable than the risky business of change.

In schools ecosystemic theory can be used to focus away from the individual and towards the system within which the individual finds him/herself. Investigation of interactions between teachers, pupils and others in the school setting shed light on the system in place, and the possible ways of altering the system. It may also be necessary to include the parents, siblings and others in this investigation. All parts of the system could be taking a share in the problem.

	Yes	No	Maybe

Humanistic psychology believes in setting up to succeed by meeting needs and enabling a person to do well.

□ □ □

Behaviouristic psychology is concerned with a person's inner feelings rather than outward expressions.

□ □ □

Behaviourism believes genetics has a big role to play in determining how we behave.

□ □ □

To be successful with people with behaviour difficulties, we need to keep reflecting on our own behaviour as well as other people's.

□ □ □

Behaviourism is concerned with our unconscious processes.

□ □ □

Behaviourism concentrates on training.

□ □ □

Cognitive behavioural psychology appreciates different people respond in different ways to stimuli and grew out of the behaviourist school of psychology.

□ □ □

The psychodynamic approach believes the origin of behavioural difficulties stems from the unconscious mind.

□ □ □

Attachment theory was born out of behaviourist thinking.

□ □ □

Difficult behaviour is often directed at someone rather than the cause of the problem.

□ □ □

Constructivist

George Kelly writing in the 1950s used the metaphor of man as a scientist, conducting experiments, constantly observing, hypothesizing, testing and reviewing according to the results he found. Kelly believed everyone constructs a model of the world like a map, and this enables them to chart their behaviour relative to the map. Over time, they will discover that their map was not initially correct, so they will adapt it to suit the findings made along the course of their journey. Personal construct psychology believes that to understand a person's behaviour it is necessary to know how that person construes a particular situation. To know this means we have to listen carefully to a person, to accept and understand their language, to suspend our judgement and get into their way of thinking. Constructivism denies the existence of an absolute truth, as each of us construct our own reality, and that is the only thing that is real – what we actually think as an individual. Constructivism offers us a way of understanding behaviour in that the behaviour we see is that person's outward manifestation of him/her making sense of his/her world.

Biological

Anyone who has brought up a child in the absence of one biological parent will be convinced biology influences behaviour. As our knowledge of genetics increases there is more and more evidence to suggest biology, or more specifically, our genetic make-up, is responsible for the way our behaviour develops, in tandem with the environment. If a person has a genetic propensity for a behavioural disorder, a stressful environment will help to bring about the manifestation of the disorder. Twin studies have supported this theory. Usually the problems are the results of neurotransmitter functioning deficiency. Neurotransmitter functioning is controlled genetically and a number of defective genes will combine to result in a problem too great for the brain to compensate for. The male brain being less able to make compensations than the female, because the female brain is better able to interchange and adapt the use of both sides of the brain for differing functions. Consequently we see more learning difficulties in boys than girls.

Other problems can be caused through endocrine dysfunctions in the form of hormonal imbalance.

It is true to say that behaviour dysfunction can be both maximized and minimized by the environment within which we find ourselves, therefore it is always worth reflecting on the environment and how we can make it more amenable to better behaviour.

Activity

Think of an environment within which you feel anxious and your behaviour becomes slightly (or very) dysfunctional.

Summary

Above are sketches of some of the theories surrounding behaviour. As stated earlier although I appreciate each theory needs to be stated and to have a definite viewpoint they are all theories and belong in the realms of academia. In practice we cherry-pick the bits that suit the situation we find ourselves in as we struggle to make sense of our world and the young people we work with. It's good to know about the theories though and there is a list for further reading at the back of this book. Essentially on a day to day basis we need to remember a few points:

- we are all trying to make sense of the world within which we find ourselves
- we are all doing the best we can with the information we have at the moment

- we all need to keep reflecting on our o well as other people's
- we are all part of systems which will behaviour and our behaviour will affect part of
- we all have different potentials for res tions, sometimes potential is affected by up, previous experience and emotional s
- always look behind the behaviour
- behaviour is a communication but is direct hit at you – it could be that you a line at the time
- we all have needs which if they are not n ability to learn
- maintaining a good sense of humour is iour management.

Chapter 1 review

Quiz

1   The humanistic approach to understanding EBD emphasizes meeting people's basic needs.

2   Abraham Maslow created a hierarchy of needs believing basic needs should be met before higher order things can be considered.

3   All behaviour is a kind of communication. Training in Neuro-Linguistic Programming enables the practitioner to calibrate behaviour and read unconscious signals.

		Yes	No	Maybe
14	Social learning theory developed from the behaviourist school and focuses on modelling.	☐	☐	☐
15	Ecosystemic theory looks at isolated acts.	☐	☐	☐
16	Biological theory attributes much behaviour to genetic components.	☐	☐	☐
17	The constructivist approach believes we all operate like scientists, testing hypotheses as we go through life and changing according to the results we find.	☐	☐	☐
18	EBD covers a narrow range of issues all to do with acting out behaviour.	☐	☐	☐
19	One of the greatest gifts for coping with difficult behaviour is a good sense of humour and the ability to laugh at yourself.	☐	☐	☐

2

Behaviour as communication

Behaviour as communication

The most important information about a person is that person's behaviour. To be able to make good use of that information we need to become very good at reading it and calibrating on it. Neuro-Linguistic Programming offers the techniques and skills to be able to do this. It does not look for deep meanings as to why a person behaves the way they do, but it does enable enhanced communication. Later in the book we will look at how you can use principles of NLP in your work in school and at home if you wish. Looking for meaning is also a key factor of psychodynamic theory from which attachment theory has evolved.

Attachment theory

Attachment theory has its origins in the work of John Bowlby (1969, 1982) who researched into the effects of disrupted childhood on adult behaviour. He believed that if a child is separated from his/her mother or primary caregiver early in life, long-standing psychological damage was a likelihood, and that a child needs to feel a loving and long-term relationship with his/her mother for good mental health. You will almost certainly have heard the term 'maternal depravation' which is the hypothesis put forward by Bowlby that breaking maternal bonds early in life has lasting and sometimes irreversible impact on a person's mental health. Bowlby suggested that children need a secure base, meaning we all like to know where we stand, we like things to be organized and to know what is expected of us. We actually need and like rules – so long as they are not ridiculously restrictive. We need freedom within a framework of discipline, otherwise we get lost and drift, not knowing where our direction is, and hence feel unsafe or insecure. We need to be able to wander from our secure base, but to feel safe in so doing, to know that we can return to a secure base when we need support, refreshment and love.

A secure base then has also been referred to by Bion (1967) as a container. The mother figure acts as this container – providing emotional holding for the child. Taking up the anxiety of the child and providing a role model of how to deal with them, not by flying off the handle, but by coping calmly and communicating understanding. Mothers take in a child's feelings, contain and synthesize them, returning them in a digestible format for the child to go away with and use. Containment though does not stop at the child-mother interface. Containment happens in all good organizations and systems that nurture and enable the people within the system to feel secure and to thrive. A good school provides emotional containment for the pupils, a good headteacher provides emotional containment for the staff, a good team leader provides emotional containment for his/her team, and so on.

Good, healthy attachment occurs when the container mother figure and the child figure can achieve a comfortable distance, not too dependent upon each other, but nonetheless secure in the knowledge that the container is there when needed. Good attachment is very dependent on the mother's ability to see the child's need – in fact the baby's need, as the attachment and bonding process takes place very early in a child's life.

As you are reading through this I'm sure you are becoming conscious of the implications of secure attachment to behaviour in the classroom. If a child feels safe and well 'attached' and 'contained', he/she will feel more able to settle down and learn.

Types of attachment – how attachment difficulties manifest themselves

Avoidant attachment

Attachment patterns were researched by Ainsworth et al in 1978, in an experiment termed the Strange Situation where video footage of children with their mother was used to analyse and categorize attachment styles. Children with an avoidant attachment style tended to avoid rather than seek contact with their mother. In the classroom a child with this style of attachment will manifest by showing indifference to anxiety in a new situation. He/she is likely to deny the need for support from the adult in the classroom but will be sensitive to their proximity. When children with avoidant attachment are engaged in a task they will tend to appear independent, autonomous and involved in the task. The task acts as an emotional safety barrier between the child and the adult in the room. The problems with this way of operating are that the child is likely to be underachieving, may have limited use of language, and limited use of creativity.

Reasons behind this behaviour are thought to be avoidance of closeness with mother because of rejection experienced. The child feels in a very difficult position because they want to be close to the adult, but also simultaneously fear rejection; it's a lose–lose situation. Understandably, anxiety will be felt because of this difficult situation.

The relationship between the child and the adult can be developed via the task. The task provides a way of avoiding the relationship with the adult and gives a focus for his attention. While this process is taking place the adult can feel left out in the cold, and if they do not understand what is going on, they could react negatively and reinforce the feelings the child has towards adults who have rejected him/her in the past.

Resistant/ambivalent attachment

A child with a resistant or ambivalent attachment pattern will be very anxious about school. He/she will be very attention-needing in regard to adults in the room. He/she will appear very dependent on the adult in the room, and will paradoxically appear hostile towards the adult. He/she will rely heavily on others to help him/her do a task, and will turn his/her attention to the fact that the adult is not attending to him/her every moment rather than getting on with the task with an element of independence. The problems associated with this child in the learning situation are that he/she is likely to be under-achieving, his/her language may be well developed because of the demand for attention and consequent adult interaction, and he/she may at times appear hostile. These children can acquire labels such as ADHD because of their severe attention-needing behaviour.

Disorganized/disorientated attachment

This group of children are what Geddes (2006) describes as the most worrying pupils. They show their difficulties in severe acting out behaviour. These children are very confusing to be with because of their inconsistent behaviour sending out mixed messages to those around. The immediate reasons behind this behaviour are thought to be that the child is in constant fear and anxiety, and that despite having a secure physical and emotional base from which to operate, still feels unable to engage with society without conflict. There is a feeling of siege, a looking out for danger, always on the edge, full of adrenalin, and no empathy with others. These children seem to have no concept of being 'held in mind'. Children like this are often described as having no ability to take criticism, often preferring to screw up any attempts at work they have done rather than accept it may be less than perfect. They may be heard saying 'what you looking at?' in an accusative tone when in fact they had not received a look that others would find threatening. There is an assumption that everyone is against them. They are half empty and away from people, as opposed to half full and forward moving. They may give off an air of knowing it all already and give no credence to the superior subject knowledge of the teacher. Not being in control of situations will be very frightening to these children and not knowing what is happening or what is going to happen will be too. Their learning and achievement will be impeded by all of this, and they will be operating at a lower level than expected for their age and perceived ability. It is almost as if you need to unlock them to allow their creativity to come out, but they are holding on tight and don't feel happy to let it flow. These young people experience overwhelming uncontained anxiety and in response exhibit acute fear and anxiety. They are very hard to understand and work with in the classroom. Possibly the only way school staff will be able to cope is to have regular and adequate supervision so that they are able to contain the anxiety and fear that spills out. (For more discussion on supervision in schools turn to Chapter 5.) These children can acquire the label of conduct disorder because of their outright oppositional behaviour.

 Activity

Write a short description of a child you have known who has displayed any of the three kinds of behaviour described above.

In the light of what you have read, can you suggest any reasons why he/she was acting in this way?

Think back to the time you were working with him/her, can you describe the feelings you felt at that time?

If I suggested to you that the feelings you were feeling were also the feelings he/she was feeling at the time, would you be able to understand what I mean?

Nurture groups

You may not have a nurture group in your school, but it is a good idea to bear in mind the theories behind nurture groups when managing groups of EBD children. A nurture group is a small class of children, usually in the primary sector, but not always, where two staff work consistently with the group, providing a secure safe base in which the young people can grow socially, emotionally and intellectually. They can gradually explore with more confidence the world around, thus increasing their learning. Nurture groups were first set up by Marjorie Boxall in London in the 1970s. (Bennathan and Boxall 2000) A traditional nurture group would take children after registration with their regular class to the nurture group, where they would then begin to prepare breakfast. The act of preparing and eating food together with two supportive adults who are modelling the role of good parents is crucial to adequate social and emotional development. After this, there would be very structured activities designed to further develop the emotional and social aspects of the children. Academic tasks take a back seat. Play is likely to be more important. For children at certain stages in their development, play is work. Missing out on the right kind of play will result in developmental delays.

A nurture group in action

Nurture Group for KS3 at Tividale Community Arts College

The KS3 Nurture Group is targeted at Year 7 and Year 8. At the time of writing there are two separate groups, one for each year group. In the beginning a pilot group was set up from Year 7. Pupils were identified in consultation with the Head of Year using information collected while the pupils were still at primary school;

Boxall profiles and observations made by support staff. Subsequent groups have been selected through consultation with Year 6 teachers with pupils attending taster nurture sessions as part of the induction process. Pupils were carefully selected to ensure a mixture of acting in and acting out pupils. Sessions are initially timetabled for a double lesson each day. From the outset it was planned to reduce the sessions after around two terms, however, pupils who made progress more quickly were encouraged to reduce their sessions earlier – where needed, nurture sessions were replaced with other individual provision. When the Year 7 group moved into Year 8 they 'graduated' into the 100 minute group. This group attended two 50 minute lessons per week.

The group is based in the Oasis Room, a room designated to nurture where there are soft chairs as well as tables and plenty of space for different activities to take place. Each day starts in a circle and pupils eat fruit and talk about how they are, but only when holding the teddy. Then they go on to do what they describe as work or activities. The work means maths, science etc. to make up for the lesson missed. Activities are more craft based or games. Following this, is a snack time where pupils work together to set the table and prepare the food. This may be toast and drinks. They sit around the table and eat together with the staff, clear away, wash up, then go on to choose an activity. The process of preparing food, eating together and tidying away afterwards is essential to the nurture process.

The group is run by three staff, of whom two are always present at any one time.

Staff report that they have seen a huge difference in the children, namely that pupils are far less withdrawn; they can now make secure attachments with adults when formerly they could not; there is an increased sense of happiness within the group; the friendship making and keeping ability has increased; there are far less tantrums and sulking sessions and pupils seem better able to contain their own emotions; co-operation has increased; they now ask for things politely; exhibit confidence; and are more able to take risks with their work, e.g. reading

aloud in class. Staff point out that the structure provided by the nurture setting is important to the success, and the elements of choice available within that setting give the children a sense of control that they otherwise may not have. In addition, attendance at school of pupils attending the group has improved as pupils now want to come to school because school now seems to have some relevance to their lives.

The children themselves report that they 'have fun; they are happy; it's better than lessons; it's sane in here; they can concentrate better in the nurture group than in lessons; have learned co-operation and how to set a table and serve up food, and how to wash up'.

Although the example above is of a well-developed nurture group with a designated space and time it may be possible to incorporate nurturing principles into the work that you as a TA are responsible for. For example, it may be possible to integrate that all-important food preparation and eating together aspect of nurture described above.

Enhancing communication using Neuro-Linguistic Programming (NLP) in the classroom

Why NLP?

Something like 10 years ago, when I first became aware of NLP for some strange reason I felt myself becoming more and more drawn to it. I wasn't sure why, but I could not deny a kind of resonance with the concepts that it seemed to be about. Looking back I can see that what we now know of as accelerated learning in education was actually out of the NLP stable. Many other concepts – learning styles, multiple intelligences, Brain Gym® also have a neurological aspect that links them with NLP. However, NLP is so much more than that. In my

experience as an advisory teacher it became clear that the basis of good teaching is a good relationship with the student, or students. The skills to build a good relationship quickly should be in the tool bag of anyone who works in a school. The basis of this skill is that of building rapport. One of the very first things you do when you attend an NLP course is an exercise in developing good rapport. Later in this chapter you will find such an exercise to try yourself. Rapport entails many things that excellent communicators do intuitively. NLP introduces the student of NLP to ways of doing this effortlessly and unconsciously. Of course it does take a bit of time to learn, but with a little practice anyone can become a better communicator and build better rapport with those you wish to. It's amazing the way a little investment in learning these things can pay dividends in the classroom, in relationships, in life. Everyone benefits.

To gain rapport then, we have to learn about the way people take information in, which senses seem to be dominant, and how they communicate by observing their preferred communication style, then practise mirroring that style, and before long you have built up a good relationship. In addition to this mirroring of the physical, we have to mirror the auditory as well: if the voice is low, we go down to meet it; if it's high, we go up there too; gradually by going where the other person goes we gain rapport and then can begin to lead and the other person will, unconsciously, follow. Think about how useful this skill could be in the classroom. Isn't it better to use a carrot than a stick? Once you have that you are able to enable your students to go further in areas they, and possibly you, never thought possible. Good education is dependent upon the relationships built up in the classroom. Think back to the teachers you remember as your favourites and who were able to inspire you to learn. Chances are they were the ones who were excellent communicators.

NLP grew out of the study of very gifted communicators. The founders of NLP, John Grinder and Richard Bandler, studied the communication styles of these people and modelled their behaviour, they found amazing and interesting results which they talk about in *The Structure of Magic: A Book About Language and Therapy* published in 1989. By modelling the way excellent communicators work, anyone can improve their communication skills, and for human beings communication is like lifeblood. Who wouldn't want to improve their communication skills?

Presuppositions of NLP

Before the rapport exercise we need to look at the cornerstones of NLP, the presuppositions of NLP. I have always found consideration of the presuppositions very useful when thinking about classroom behaviour and the behaviour of EBD children in general. See what you think.

People are not their behaviours – accept the person, change the behaviour. This presupposition always makes me think of the quotation from Mahatma Gandhi: 'Hate the sin, love the sinner.' It is a very useful thought to hold on to when coping with people exhibiting difficult and challenging behaviour, particularly when it seems to be directed at YOU! If we can keep the distinction in mind that people are far more than the behaviour they are showing us right now, it gives us the strength to persevere. Remember also that by using rapport building techniques you will be able to take a person with you and help them to change their behaviour. You are not powerless, every reaction you experience is just that – a reaction – and you are instrumental in creating what comes to you. If things seem as though they are not going the way you want them to go, you need to step back, think, change tactic and project what you want to receive.

'The map is not the territory.' This is a quotation from Alford Korzybski who developed general semantics theory. He believed that a map should not be confused with the territory it represents, it is simply that – a representation of the territory. The map is very useful as a guide, but it is not the real thing – it differs in many ways – it's on paper, it's scaled down, its colours differ to that which it represents. Of course this is just a metaphor, and the real meaning is that each one of us has our own map in our mind of the reality 'out there', i.e. the environment we find ourselves in. We understand reality according to our map. We need this map and could not function without it, but we need to remember that maps from time to time need to be redrafted when we discover a new bit of 'reality'. Our senses take in raw data from our environment and that raw data has absolutely no meaning whatsoever other than the meaning we choose to give it. Korzybski illustrated this in a lecture by going to his bag and explaining he needed a biscuit, he offered the biscuits around, some students took the biscuits, he then revealed the packaging more fully – dog biscuits – the reaction from some of the students when they believed they had eaten dog biscuits was to feel sick. He said this proved people do not only eat food, they eat words too. The meaning then, that we as individuals attribute to situations, is immensely powerful. We can use that to our advantage, or disadvantage, the choice is ours.

Body and mind are systemic processes – mind and body are part of the same cybernetic system. Anything happening in the mind also happens in the body and vice versa. This has particular implications on our body language. We all give off unconscious signals that other people's unconscious minds pick up on. We will then elicit more unconscious communication and sometimes we wonder why someone has behaved towards us in the way they have, when in fact, if we could just understand these unconscious signals we would not be half as perplexed. On a conscious level if we act as if we are pleased to see someone, our mind will respond to that and begin to be more kindly disposed to that person. Sometimes we need to get our body to go through the motions of something – to get it in the muscle, and then we actually begin to really feel those feelings inside. In the context of health, Deepak Chopra has written a lot on how the mind and emotions affect the body's healing systems (*Quantum Healing*: 1989).

Every behaviour is useful in some context – no behaviour is wrong in itself, it is perhaps just not the most appropriate behaviour for the context. As we go about our business as human beings, we are trying to make sense of the world and do the best we can. Essentially everyone wants to be happy, we all seek pleasure, sometimes though the way we get that pleasure will be contrary to someone else, and may cause significant harm. Nonetheless, to the doer, it makes some kind of sense. It is worth appreciating that when working with challenging behaviour. You will remember the section on attachment theory, how some behaviours really seem to be very contrary and go against making the life of anyone, doer or done to, any better, but look behind and you may find some kind of meaning, because there is sure to be meaning in there. This presupposition does not give excuses or negations for bad behaviour, it just helps us to find reasons and, once we have found reasons for our behaviour, we can work towards moving away from negative behaviour patterns. Also, when we know a person's motivation, we can tune into that, and appeal to their motivation to elicit good behaviour rather than negative behaviour.

The meaning of your communication is the response that you get – it does not matter what you meant, what matters is what actually results from your words, tone and actions. How many times have you said to someone, 'I didn't mean it like *that*!'

The fact is though in the other person's reality, *that* is exactly what you did mean, because *that* is the way he/she took it. It comes back to the difference between the map and the territory again. We have to accept that other people might not construe something the way we do, so as great communicators, we need to look again, listen to what they are saying, listen to how they are saying it, tune in, get rapport, get into their skin, and communicate using their ways. That way we have a bigger chance of speaking the same language. The only person we really have any control over changing is ourselves, so if our message is not getting across and having the affect we think it should have, we need to change the way we are acting. If we try to change someone else without changing the way we respond to that person first, we will always get what we have always got from them.

There is no failure only feedback – all results are useful information and can be used to propel us to success. Now you have adopted this mind-shift you will see how much more positive the whole world is. The great thing about this too is that you can use it so much with the young people you work with. Just by using the terminology you will be setting up more positive thinking about the self in the mind of the young person. By asking 'what's the feedback?' and then going through this as a positive piece of information which can be built on, you can really help young people to grow in self esteem and confidence. In addition, it is a good idea to talk about feedback you have received during your week. It may be that you have had some feedback from one of your own family members, friends or colleagues which it is OK to talk about. By doing this, you model that it is normal to receive feedback throughout your life, and that you welcome it and use it to help you to do things differently next time if necessary. It may be that some of the young people you work with don't often see adults around them coping well with feedback.

The person with the most flexibility and choices of behaviour will rule the system – in order to get different results, you need to keep doing different things. If you always do what you have always done, you'll always get what you've always got. You may have some colleagues or friends who always seem to know what to do in a difficult situation (you might be lucky enough to consider yourself to be one of these people). The chances are that they use a number of strategies, and that these strategies cover quite a range. These people will be flexible in their approach, they will be unflappable, not fazed by any situation they find themselves in, and probably appear quietly confident. They will be good communicators who are able to read unconscious signals, and adapt to the communication styles of others and to any situation they find themselves in. Contrast this with people who are rigid and will not bend on anything. They are at a distinct disadvantage when trying to communicate well with others because their comfort range is so narrow that a lot of communication opportunities will fall outside of their range and, consequently, be lost. In your role as a TA, you need to be an excellent communicator, not only with the young people you work with, but with the teachers and the parents. You will need to be flexible in the way you communicate and, if you are, you will have a good picture of how things are from three different perspectives.

There are no resistant clients only inflexible communicators – something will work and if you look deep enough and try enough things you will very likely find something that works. The word 'client' here might sound a bit off-putting, but if you can think in terms of the client being the child it might make more sense. In our role as the adult around the child, we need to keep trying to find ways to communicate effectively with the child so that the response we get from our communication is the one we want to get. If we get a different one, we need to find another way. In Greek mythology, Procrustes had an iron bed onto which he invited guests to lie down. If the guest proved too tall, he would cut off their legs, if the guest was too short, he was stretched out on it until he fit. If we want to behave like Procrustes we can expect everyone else to fit our standard. However, it would seem more sensible to try to adapt and maybe have a bed that can be more accommodating. (In fact Procrustes used to secretly adjust the bed when he saw the size of the guest ensuring a bloody end every time. Fortunately Theseus put a stop to all of this by putting Procrustes in the bed prepared for Theseus – a short stout fellow – so Procrustes lost his head and feet.)

Resistance is a sign of lack of rapport – we will move heaven and earth for those we love and want to impress. When you have rapport you have massive influence. Sometimes in our work we need to act as if we really love the young people we work with, even when we feel we don't. During my training, my mother – a retired head teacher – used to say to me, 'You have to love your children.' She is right, if you want to get the best out of them you have to really value and cherish them. If you take time to get rapport, to get into the way they are thinking, you will find communicating and leading them through learning so much easier. If they resist you, go back and look at **your** rapport skills. Think about what you need to do to put them at their ease, to level with them and to make them feel you accept them for what and who they are, that you are meeting them where they are, not where you want them to be. You will know when you have rapport, you can just feel it; things change. It's as if you were swimming around in the sea and suddenly, instead of swimming some distance away from each other, you start swimming alongside each other, going along together smoothly, making progress in unison. Your movement in the water creates mutually helpful currents, it becomes a symbiotic experience.

All genius, excellence and amazing achievement has structure and a strategy, and for this reason it can be learned. When I was training to be a teacher I remember one of our tutors advising us to watch good teachers and model what they do. From a very early age we watch what other people do and we start to copy their actions. Initially we don't think consciously about what we are doing. As babies our unconscious mind will be taking us through these actions. Gradually we work out what effect things have and we build on the learning. Have you ever noticed how sometimes when we are trying to learn how to do something we actually get worse at it as we start to think too hard about it. In NLP we need to get into the 'know nothing state', or the 'alpha state' before we start to model another person. This means as far as possible we empty our mind, a bit like meditation, and then copy the skill we want to achieve.

We have all the resources we need. All the resources we need are inherent in our own physiology and neurology. This is such an empowering idea to hold on to. Think about children and adults you know who keep making excuses as to why they can't do something. Often they will try to make you believe that circumstances beyond their control are stopping them from doing things, and this is a convincing argument that you might really go along with for a long time. In fact you might even do a little bit of this yourself. Think though for a minute how it would feel to truly believe that you can affect your own success. One of the great things about NLP is that is opens your mind up to new possibilities. You cast away limiting beliefs that have been holding you back for years and years and become open to success. Each one of us has what we need to succeed.

We create our own experience and therefore we are responsible for what happens to us. This presupposition leads on from the last. Once we can accept that we have the resources we need, it is only one small step to move into making things happen that we want to happen. If we don't make something happen that we have decided we want, and we still really want it, we need to go back, look at what we are doing, and do it differently. If it isn't working, change the way we do it. Look at the way successful people operate in this field, what are they doing that you aren't. Is there something you could learn from someone else?

Calibrate behaviour – the most important information about a person is that person's behaviour. This is so useful in the classroom. To be able to understand a person we need to develop sensory acuity and calibrate the behaviour of others. Not everyone behaves in the same way when they are angry, sad, happy, etc. To stereotype body language can be very misleading and lead to poor communication. Little unconscious signals, tiny twitches of fingers, eyebrows, eye movements, breathing fluctuations, lip shapes, lines round the mouth, are all signals that we can consciously tune into; we can become much much better at reading how people are thinking, and then we have the opportunity to introduce an idea at a point when they are receptive to it. Isn't that something you would like to learn more about?

The first area for exploration in NLP is building rapport. To do this is very easy, but takes practice to hone the skill to a fine art. It is really useful when you find yourself faced with someone who is making you feel rather uneasy, and who could be coming across as a little aggressive. In fact, whatever state the other person is in, if you aren't intuitively in rapport with him/her you can increase the volume of your rapport building and bring him/her along with you. I was on a course recently and was faced with a fellow delegate who was coming across as very aggressive in his approach. Soon I had an opportunity to sit next to him. I matched the movements and positions he was making with his body, I matched the tone of voice and size of phrases he was speaking, and very soon he was listening to my point of view and we started getting on very well. He visibly relaxed and the aggressive, negative side disappeared for the rest of the day. I felt good, he felt good. We were congruent and helping each other get the best out of the day.

Building rapport – matching and mirroring

Mirroring is physically 'copying', as if in a mirror, the behaviour of another person. This needs to be done with respect and subtlety or will look false and silly; however, do not be afraid to try – it really does work – and to begin with you can practise with a friend who won't mind you copying their every movement. In a real-world situation, the person with whom you are communicating will unconsciously feel acknowledged and appreciate your interest in them, and it will have a profound effect.

Matching can have a short time delay, but is very similar to mirroring in other respects. If someone is making a movement whilst talking and explaining a point, you can be attentive, then as soon as it is your turn to speak you use a similar kind of gesture to explain your point. Unconsciously you are recognised as someone who understands and 'speaks my language' so you will be listened to more intently. You can also do some cross-over matching which means using a corresponding but slightly different behaviour to match, like finger tapping in time with rapid blinking.

Practising these skills enables you to observe other people in more and more detail. You will build up trust and your ability to lead children in learning will be enhanced.

Rapport activity

You can try doing a rapport exercise for yourself by following the instructions below. You will need two other people to help you practise this.

- Person A begins to tell person B about a work or personal experience. Person C watches. A and B and will comment later on what they were doing.

- C needs to be watching for all of the things described below, so please read the notes fully.
- B matches and mirrors (as described above) A by making the same kind of movements as A. Remember to look for where the eyes go too and follow this movement. You are in a conversation, so contribute to the conversation, try to match their style of talking; if they use lots of visual language, you use visual language too; if they use auditory, you use auditory. Also, look out for the chunk sizes of the pieces of information they are offering to you. Match the size of information you give to the size they are giving you. This feels strange to begin with, and it is true you are in a false situation, but try to go along with this as so much of NLP is about 'getting it in the muscle', so your kinesthetic memory can automatically bring the behaviour patterns back up when necessary. If you haven't done it, you can't expect your memory to remember it, can you?
- As you are doing all of this, notice feelings of comfort and discomfort as they occur.
- Notice what is going on internally in your body as well as externally.
- Totally establish rapport. You will notice when you are in rapport. You will feel easier. Notice FEELINGS as you gain rapport.
- Also look for outward signs of rapport.
- Develop now involving matching the voice – try to match tone, volume and intonation.
- Don't forget to match breathing as well.

How did that feel?

Discuss with your two friends and swap over roles.

In a real-life situation the other person is not aware that you are trying to establish rapport. It just happens to him/her and they feel easier. So in real life, once you have become consciously aware of the skills yourself it is much much easier than doing it in a false situation like this. You can try this with family members if it is easier, or even do it with some children, after all what better skills can you teach them than excellent communication?

Sensory activity

You will need another person to help you with this activity, but again you could try it out with your pupils.

Ask the other person to think of something they like a lot. You can suggest they say what they saw when they last saw this thing, smell what they smelled, feel what they felt.

While they are recalling this lovely thing, notice the expressions; skin colour; skin tone, etc.

	Like	*Dislike*
Eyes		
Lip size		
Lip shape		
Head position		
Breathing rate		
Breathing position		
Foot position		

	Like	*Dislike*
Hand position		
Skin colour		
Skin tone		
Any twitches		
Facial expressions		
General comments		

Now, in the same way ask them to think of something they dislike intensely.

Make the same observations.

Now ask the person to choose which one they wish to think about so that we can guess which one it is.

What did you notice about the unconscious signs?

You can heighten your awareness in all sensory areas. Here is an auditory way to do this:

.

Auditory sensitivity exercise

You will need three people altogether to practise this exercise, A, B and C. A closes their eyes. B and C make similar sounds in the same location in a space behind A (sounds can be clicking fingers, clapping, rubbing palms together) immediately followed by their own name. Continue doing this until A feels they can identify which sound belongs to which person. Test by A calling out the name of the person they feel has made the sound immediately they make it. Guessing quickly will make this task easier – let your unconscious mind do the work.

In a similar way you will be able to tune into the tone of a person's voice, even when they are trying hard to hide their feelings, and be able to tell if they are happy about a situation or something you are asking them to do, or not. If they are not, you are setting yourself up to fail and need to go back, look at how you have been communicating and try another approach. This is very empowering as it gives the control back to you. You can do something about negative situations.

Representational System Language

We all have sensory preferences when we are communicating with others. For some time now the awareness in schools of the different learning styles of children has been gathering momentum. Ideally we all need things presented to us in a variety of ways to give learning the best possible chance to take place. Some are very visual people, some prefer auditory, some very tactile, or kinesthetic. A good communicator will tune in to the preferred communication style by taking note of the representational language and use that as a kind of dialect to enable enhanced communication. This is easy to do once you have raised your awareness of the different styles and learned how to speak the same dialect as others. You will be amazed at how much more easily you can get your message across.

Activity – Ascertaining representational system language – can you see, hear and feel what I mean?

A, B and C.

A ask B the following questions. Both A and C listen clearly for all sensory language used by B, and write each one down as they say it. You will notice that there are essentially four questions, but after each one I have added an extra question to try to draw out more thinking. Sometimes, because of the falseness of the situation, it is hard for people to free up on the answers, so asking the extra questions stated here will help them to keep talking without you putting words into their mouth.

B – Forget about what you are doing and try to answer the questions as naturally and honestly and deeply and congruently as you can. Close your eyes if it will help you.

1. This morning how did you make up your mind about what clothes to wear today?
2. Is there anything else you do?
3. Tell me why you do your favourite hobby?
4. Yes, tell me a bit more about that.
5. When you are really tired, how do you motivate yourself to get up in the morning?
6. Do you do anything else?
7. How do you know when it's time to take a break and do something fun?
8. Do you do that every time, or do you sometimes do something else?

Remember, you are not interested in the actual answers. The context is irrelevant. Just listen carefully for language that indicates visual, auditory or kinesthetic preferences. All you are looking for here is to see where B goes to find the information you have requested.

Change roles and each have a turn in each position.

Categorization of words in representational system

The tables of words and phrases below give an idea of how to categorize words into representational systems. You may not agree with all of them, but you will see a pattern emerging as you read through. You may also feel more in tune with one column than others. Have a read through and find out.

Visual	Auditory	Kinesthetic
Admire	Answer	Beat
Attractive	Argue	Bends
Blurred	Asked	Brush
Bright	Call	Burdened
Cloudy	Chatter	Carry
Colourful	Cry	Clumsy
Conceal	Discuss	Concrete
Enlighten	Echo	Cowering
Expose	Growl	Hurt
Eyed	Gurgling	Immoveable
Foggy	Harmonize	Movement
Glance	Hear	Numb
Glimpse	Hum	Pressure
Glitzy	Melodious	Pull
Graphic	Mumble	Push
Hazy	Noisy	Scrape
Illuminate	Overtones	Shaky
Look	Quiet	Slip
Obscure	Resonance	Smooth
Observe	Sang	Solid
Peer	Screaming	Spiky
Perspective	Shrill	Stuffed
Preview	Silent	Sweep
Reflect	Sounds	Thick
See	Tell	Touchy
Staring	Translate	Trample
Twinkle	Undertones	Twist
View	Unhearing	Unfeeling
Visualize	Vocal	Weigh

Sensory predicate phrases

Visual	Auditory	Kinesthetic
An eyeful	A little bird told me	All washed up
Appears to me	All ears	An uphill climb
Bird's eye view	An earful	Boils down to
Catch a glimpse of	Be heard	Catch my drift
Clear cut	Blabber mouth	Catch on
Clear image	Call on	Chip off the old block
Clear view	Clear as a bell	Come to grips with
Crystal clear	Clearly expressed	Connect with
Eye to eye	Describe in detail	Control yourself
Flashed on	Express yourself	Cool/calm/collected
Get a perspective	Give account of	Firm foundations
Get scope on	Give me your ear	Floating on air
Hazy idea	Grant me an audience	Get a handle on
Horse of a different colour	Heard voices	Get a hold of
I get the picture	Hidden messages	Get a load of this
In light of	Hold your tongue	Get in touch with
In person	Idle talk	Hand in hand
In view of	I hear you	Hang in there
I see what you mean	Inquire into	Heated argument
Looks good to me	Loud and clear	Hold it
Make a scene	Make music	I catch your drift
Mental picture	Out of synch	It feels right to me
Mind's eye	Outspoken	Make contact
Paint a picture	Power of speech	Pain in the neck
Photographic	Purrs like a kitten	Plain sailing
Plainly seen	Rings a bell	Pull some strings
Pretty as a picture	State your purpose	Sharp as a tack
See to it	Sounds like	Slipped my mind
Short sighted	That clicks	Smooth operator
Showing off	To tell the truth	Start from scratch
Sight for sore eyes	Tune in/tune out	Tap into
Take a dim view	Unheard of	Touch on
Take a look	Utterly	Treading on thin ice
Tunnel vision	Voice an opinion	Walk through

Translation between representational styles

Look at the sentences below and see how differently the same situation can be matched using the same representational style, and how they can be described in different representational styles.

Example 1. My future looks hazy

Match: **Visual:** When I look to the future, it doesn't seem clear.

Translate: **Auditory:** I can't tune in to my future.

Kinesthetic: I can't get a feel for what seems to be going to happen.

Example 2. Zoe doesn't listen to me

Match: **Auditory:** Zoe goes deaf when I talk.

Translate: **Visual:** Zoe never sees me, even when I'm right in front of her eyes.

Kinesthetic: I get the feeling Zoe doesn't even try to catch my drift.

Example 3. Gemma gets churned up when the head expects her planning

Match: **Kinesthetic:** Gemma gets agitated and tense over submitting her planning

Translate: **Visual:** Gemma goes blind crazy and her vision fogs up when her planning becomes due.

Auditory: Gemma's ears ring because she has to face the music if her planning isn't in on time.

You can now go on to use this knowledge when you are working with young people. Speak in their representational style and you will be more understood.

	Yes	No	Maybe
secure boundaries.	☐	☐	☐
by their mother may attachment patterns.	☐	☐	☐
erson's representational slating from your system to s will help build trust and	☐	☐	☐
rovide emotional contain- taff and pupils.	☐	☐	☐

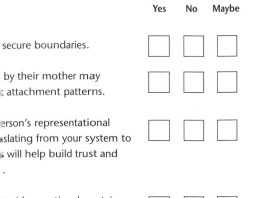

Activity

Choose a child you work with and listen to the types of words he/she uses. You will notice he/she will probably use all types of the visual, auditory and kinesthetic words, but one type will usually predominate. Then practise translating your language to his/her system.

If he/she says, 'I don't see what you mean', don't say, 'Let me repeat it', instead say, 'Let me show you what I mean.'

If he/she says, 'What you're saying doesn't feel right to me', don't say, 'Take a different view', instead say, 'Let's walk through these points another way.'

Keep practising! You will become more and more aware of how other people think, and more flexible in how you respond, and you are right now developing excellent communication skills.

Communication with parents and carers

As a parent, a teacher and a coach I have been able to observe interactions from a number of perspectives. I remember working with a teacher once who was having difficulty with a particular parent. It is true, she was a difficult mum to handle, but it was also true that the teacher was making the situation a whole lot worse by NOT LISTENING to the point of view of the parent. In your role as TA, you are unlikely to have very hostile situations to deal with, but you may have parents coming to you complaining about the teachers you work with. At these times you will need to remain very professional and neither agree nor disagree, but allow the parent to talk and unravel their story. I always found the best way to diffuse difficult situations was to sit them down and ask how I could help; questions and phrases like:

- Now, tell me about the situation
- Yes, go on

57

■ OK, leave it with me. I'll see what I can do and I'll get back to you by . . .

■ So, let me just check what you are feeling (reiterate what they have said)

■ I can't guarantee anything, but I will look into it for you

■ There is always something that can be done, but I'm not sure what it is yet.

It's all about giving people confidence, without promising you can sort it out in just the way they want it sorted, and don't forget you are also buying time. Never expect to be able to sort something out there and then when a parent comes in with a problem, it isn't the right time. At that time all you can expect to do is gather information, then you can go away and look at different perspectives. Remember too to employ all of the NLP skills you have read about – build rapport, match and mirror, get the trust of the parent.

Summary

■ Nurture groups allow children to operate at a developmentally appropriate level.

■ When people are like each other they like each other.

■ When you like someone you are willing to assist them get what they want. Most communication is outside our conscious awareness.

■ As master communicator, you will communicate best with people when you use their representational system.

■ You will know when you are in rapport, you will feel congruent, movements will mirror and match – you can begin to lead and they will follow your movements, you may feel a mild sense of anticipation or nervousness, you may feel a sense of warmth, you may feel you have known this person all your life and they likewise.

Chapter 2 rev

Quiz

1 A nurture grou
   three children

2 Preparing and
   supportive ad
   of good parer
   group activity

3 Children are r
   and how they
   group.

4 Rapport is sor
   don't – you c

5 Nurture grou

6 Nurture grou
   children of se

7 Training in N
   enables you t
   scious signals
   better.

8 In NLP we ur
   their own ve
   to accept it v

9 Mirroring pe

10 Attachment
   John Bowlby

11 Children res

12 A child rejec
   exhibit avoi

13 Finding out
   system and
   another pers
   communica

14 Good schoo
   ment for the

3

Discipline strategies

Knowing which battles to fight

The art of keeping discipline is being ahead of whomever you want to discipline in your thinking and actions. Many situations cause discipline problems simply because of poor planning. For good discipline you need to ensure that the child is in a situation where they feel safe. We can return to Maslow's hierarchy of needs here. Discipline problems usually arise from anxiety, situations where people do not feel safe, and the primitive brain steps in with fight or flight responses. Active disciplining of children is at times necessary. I make a distinction between active disciplining and implicit discipline. Ideally obvious acts of disciplining should be very few and far between. Where the system itself provides a framework of discipline which enables freedom to act within it, where the system is set up well and harmonious, with everyone's need being met, the need for people to act out and require disciplining to keep within the accepted social norms of the group will be minimal. Sometimes though, the needs of the children we are working with are extreme and do from time to time fall outside the capability of the system within which they find themselves. So they let you know their needs aren't being met, that they are feeling anxious and insecure without boundaries and uncontained (as described in the section on attachment), by acting out, possibly by a verbal, physical or emotional attack on you. Knowing which battles to fight in the discipline game will make life a lot more bearable. Some battles are just not worth fighting and should be allowed to pass, but note that you are getting feedback on the system you operate all of the time, so use that feedback to tweak the system so that the opportunity for the behaviour you don't want to see is minimized. Look at what might be causing increased anxiety, are there any ways this could be minimized? Taking the attitude that a person ought to be able to cope with a situation because everyone else does is really not helpful, but nonetheless one that we often hear. We all have to face what we are and how we cope with situations and at certain times in our life we need to keep away from certain situations and do more of others if we are able to succeed somewhere. We can gradually grow in strength and develop new capabilities, but this won't happen if we are set up to fail. Other behaviours require negotiation and compromise; they are an opening for discussion, development, feedback and growth. They are an opportunity for you to find out the other's perspective, and for them to find out yours. They are an opportunity for problem solving and much good can come of them. I once heard it said that conflict is the greatest free resource. If not the greatest, it is probably second only to love. There are still other behaviours that are so dangerous that they have to be an 'absolutely not!' There is no negotiation here. I like to think of these three types of behaviour as green, amber and red. Green – let it go, amber – compromise, red – absolutely not. Realistically there are very few absolutely nots in the classroom.

Activity – Traffic lights for behaviour

Photocopy the pages below and cut up the cards so that each behaviour is separate.

On the traffic light page sort the cards into the different coloured lights, deciding whether each behaviour is a 'let it go', 'compromise' or 'absolutely not!' As you do this activity, picture yourself in the classroom with the child and try to recall the feelings you feel in those situations.

– Physiological

	Yes	No
[H]e child had enough to eat today?	☐	☐
[H]e child recently had a drink of water?	☐	☐
[H]e child had enough sleep in the last 24 hours?	☐	☐
[Is] child constipated?	☐	☐
[Is] child suffering from any illness that makes him/her [g]enerally uncomfortable?	☐	☐

– Safety

	Yes	No
[Does] the child feel safe in school? (Is he/she scared of [someon]e or any situation in school?)	☐	☐
[Does] the child feel safe within his/her family? (Is he/she [suffer]ing abuse or neglect? Is the family breaking up?)	☐	☐
[Does] the child feel happy about the health of his/her [family] members? (Is anyone close to him/her ill at the [mom]ent?)	☐	☐
[Does] the child feel safe about his/her home? (Are the [family] about to be evicted?)	☐	☐

– Love/belonging

	Yes	No
[Does] the child have a friend in school?	☐	☐
[Does] the child feel he/she belongs in his/her school?	☐	☐
[Does] the child experience comradeship when he/she [i]s in school?	☐	☐
[Does] anyone hold him/her in mind at school so that [when] he/she comes in he/she knows someone has been [thinki]ng about him/her when he/she was not there?	☐	☐
[Does] he/she have anyone in school who has a true [under]standing of his/her needs and works hard to try to [meet] them?	☐	☐

Those feelings may, if you don't look at them and accept them for what they are – your own emotional responses – colour where you put the behaviours. Try to think rationally about the actual behaviour and what the worst thing that could happen would be as a result of this behaviour. That may help to get it into perspective.

Tells you he hates you	Will not enter the room to work
Shows anger and frustration at tasks	Rips up his own work
Runs out of the classroom	Refuses to do set task
Uses bad language in the classroom	Keeps moving around the room using different seats
Slaps another child	Sits away from the rest of the group but does work
Talks to neighbour, off task	Swings on seat, but is on task
Frequently shouting out	Keeps asking the same question of you

Refuses to pack up when everyone else is	Does not speak
Stops engaging in task as soon as you move away from him	Knows what to do without your help – but doesn't really
Cuts hair of another child	Taunts other children by pinching them, moving their stuff, sniggering
Sits under table and refuses to move	Climbs on table and dances
Runs round room turning tables over and throwing chairs	Makes no eye contact with you or anyone else

Green – let it go

Amber – compromise

Red – absolutely not!

Second

Activity – How behaviou

Taking the behaviours from th
card write the emotions or fee
with that behaviour in the classroom. You w
to feel what you felt, see what you saw, hear
you smelled; all of the senses will help you to
feeling.

Earlier in the book in the section on at
reflect on behaviour and consider tha
feeling were also the feelings the child
fact these feelings get transferred from
The hurting will tend to pass on their
can become more and more sensitive t
better able to empathize with how the
room, and that will help you to worl
that pain and enabling the needs to be
can learn – which is what they are supp
isn't it?

Activity – Needs audit

The needs audit below is one c
archy of needs.

Choose two children in the class you wor
performs very well in school and another E
audit and compare the findings. What does
should be concentrating our efforts on in sc
these children?

Need

Has th

Has tl

Has tl

Is the

Is the

feel g

Need

Does

anyor

Does

suffer

Does

family

mom

Does

family

Need

Does

Does

Does

arrive

Does

when

think

Does

unde

meet

	Yes	No

Does he/she get the feeling when he/she has been away that he/she has been missed for the right reasons – i.e. not because it has been quiet and peaceful while he/she was away but because his/her lively/kind/lateral thinking/problem solving personality was missed?

Inspired by Maslow's Hierarchy of Needs

De-escalating difficult situations

Difficult situations rarely happen completely out of the blue, in fact if you practise your skills in calibrating on behaviour as described earlier you will become so aware of unconscious signals that you will agree difficult situations never come without warning, but you do need to know your subject. As stated earlier, anxiety is the first factor in setting up a difficult situation. So, if you want a difficult situation to occur, make someone anxious. How do we do this? We can ridicule; insult them in some way; take away a favourite toy they feel gives them security; act moodily with them so they find it difficult to read our signals; change the programme at a moment's notice; shout; accuse them of something; ask them to do something they don't feel comfortable with, not to mention the possibility of things that have happened in the past that are still there in the unconscious mind just waiting for a trigger to set them off again. All of these can happen in a classroom so anxiety can arise at anytime with a vulnerable child who is not resilient enough to be able to shake off the anxiety. The signs for anxiety coming on may be things like increased agitation – finger tapping; pacing; wringing hands together; staring. The better you know the person the more signs you will notice. Some people start to emit odours, twitch, etc. Your role is to remain non-judgemental at this time. You don't necessarily know what has caused the anxiety, and it would be wrong of

67

you to make judgements; it may be something that would make you very anxious too. In addition if you can remain non-judgemental you are in a much better position to be able to support when necessary. If the anxiety spreads to you, your emotional state will blur your ability to cope. At this point the child has not yet become irrational, so you may be able to offer support and turn the situation round by using supportive language and matching the state the child is in. Remember the rapport exercise you did earlier in the book? You need to get to where they are so that they can feel real communication. This doesn't mean you lose your cool, but if you talk in a reeeeaaaly slooow way and they are all up high, they aren't going to be able to wait for you to get your words out and you will lose them. Remember to match and mirror, gain rapport. When diffusing situations it is essential to remain aware it is not just what you say, but the way that you say it.

Following the anxious stage, if you haven't managed to talk the child down, then it could be that you are faced with the defensive stage where the child begins to get argumentative and irrational. At this point you will need to be firm and set clear boundaries stating clearly and simply what the boundaries are, giving the positive choice first, then the negative one, and always make sure they are reasonable and enforceable.

It is important at all times to remain calm and continue to believe that the behaviour is not directed at you personally. This will help you to remain rational yourself and be able to continue containing the situation. If the child asks you challenging questions you need to give a rational response, divert from the challenge to the task and ignore the challenge but not the child. Don't make the mistake sometimes seen of ignoring the child and making the gulf between you and them even bigger. Always remember you ignore the behaviour, when the behaviour is appropriate you accept it as valid communication. The child may want to say more, and you need to listen well. Listening well is something in short supply in quite a few educational establishments. We want children to listen to us for a long time, but how good are we as adults at listening to them? To listen well requires achieving rapport; the suspension of judgement mentioned earlier; the giving of undivided attention; listening carefully to the feelings as well as the facts; building in time for reflection; reiteration of the message to clarify meaning. The Chinese symbol for 'to listen' is a beautiful reminder of how we need to use our ears, eyes, heart and undivided attention when we listen.

ears

eyes

heart

to give undivided attention

In addition to the things we say, we also need to look at the way we act physically when we are dealing with difficult situations. We all know that when someone squares up to us it feels aggressive and threatening and is likely to inflame a situation. Standing slightly sideways on is a much less aggressive and more supportive way to stand. When you first enter a difficult situation try to bear this in mind and use the rapport building skills as well as maintaining a non-aggressive stance.

Communicating assertively not aggressively

How do you do assertive?

In NLP language we ask, 'How do you do . . . (whatever it is we are concerned about)?' Hence the question 'How do you do assertive?' You could also ask, 'How do you do aggressive?' By looking at how we do things rather than trying to explain what we are trying to achieve or where we want to be using this action, we can look at the action itself and begin to think about ways of doing things differently. After all, the main information most people get from us is our behaviour, so whatever we think we are communicating may not be what they are actually seeing. Below I'm going to explain the differences between assertive, aggressive, passive/aggressive and passive behaviour. Then I will suggest an exercise for you to do that could help you identify these different types of behaviour.

Assertiveness

Acting assertively means you express yourself and your wishes in a way that does not violate the rights of others. Firm, fair, open, direct and honest are words that would describe assertive communication. Being assertive in negotiations usually involves discussion and compromise where a win-win situation is the most desirable outcome, but the winning may not be exactly what you had in mind at the beginning of the conversation. Being assertive does not mean you get your way no matter what, that is more like aggression. An assertive person will be willing to listen to the viewpoint of another. It may be that he/she has a valid point and that, in fact, the situation could be made much better if his/her view were taken into account.

Aggressive

Being aggressive means you try to dominate others and impose your will on them without regard to their view. When people act aggressively they do not care about another's personal boundaries, and will do all they need to make another person submit to their view.

An aggressively acting person will not consider a compromise to be a good result. He/she is likely to want it all their way or, if he/she does seem to accept a compromise, it may be that he/she is behaving in a passive/aggressive manner. Passive/aggressive is when a person goes silent, refuses to do certain things, may appear very polite and inoffensive, may use sarcasm, be plotting and spying a chance to act, or just hoping that refusal to comply will back the other person into a corner so that he/she complies with their wishes after all.

Passive

People who communicate passively have problems defending their own personal boundaries. An aggressively acting person will be able to invade these boundaries and unduly influence them. A passively acting person is likely to put his/her own needs behind those of others too often and become anxious and withdrawn as a result. He/she is likely to be quiet and unable to speak up for him/herself.

You will see that these different types of behaviour are very pertinent to the EBD child. Some EBD children are very passive, others very aggressive, others passive/aggressive, but possibly not many are what we would term truly assertive. We are all a mixture of all types of the above behaviours, but some are far less assertive than others. As adults in the classroom we can sometimes slip away from being assertive and go into the other modes of behaviour; our role though should be to maintain being as assertive as we can and lead by example.

Activity – How do you do (assertive, aggressive, passive/aggressive, passive?)

Copy the grid below and complete.
If you want to see a completed grid, go to the back of the book.

What do you do when you do . . .	. . . assertive	. . . aggressive	. . . passive/ aggressive	. . . passive
What don't you do when you do . . .	. . . assertive	. . . aggressive	. . . passive/ aggressive	. . . passive
What are the non-verbal clues when you are . . .	. . . assertive	. . . aggressive	. . . passive/ aggressive	. . . passive
What are the verbal clues when you are . . .	. . . assertive	. . . aggressive	. . . passive/ aggressive	. . . passive

- Ignoring the behaviour is not the same as ignoring the child.
- Assertive communication involves compromise and negotiation.
- Talking to yourself positively can be a great aid to confidence and something you can teach your pupils by modelling.
- Always remember to keep your sense of humour.

Chapter 3 review

Quiz

		Yes	No	Maybe
1	Discipline problems usually arise from anxiety because physiological, safety and belonging needs are not being met.	☐	☐	☐
2	It is better not to allow the feelings of a child to affect how you feel in a situation.	☐	☐	☐
3	Abraham Maslow believed children can learn without having their safety needs met.	☐	☐	☐
4	You can always predict difficult situations arising.	☐	☐	☐
5	Rapport can be used to good effect to gain information about a person's behaviour.	☐	☐	☐
6	Being an assertive communicator means you always end up getting your way.	☐	☐	☐
7	Children can learn assertive communication styles from adults in school.	☐	☐	☐
8	Listening requires periods of silence.	☐	☐	☐

		Yes	No	Maybe
9	The broken record technique is a passive way of communicating.	☐	☐	☐
10	Using positive self talk is a great way to boost confidence to do things we feel unsure about.	☐	☐	☐

Individual strategies in the learning environment

In this chapter are descriptions of several strategies that can be considered for use with individual young people. The questionnaire below is designed to help you to look both at the behaviour of the child and the environment within which they operate. By looking at these aspects together it could shed light onto some of the causes of anxiety at the root of the behaviour. If a child is of secondary age and taught by a number of teachers, the questionnaire needs to be completed by all of them because each teacher's environment will create a different situation for the child to deal with.

Looking at the child within the learning environment

Behaviour and learning environment questionnaire

Re: ....   Class...............   YG ....

Date ....

Subject .... (if applicable)

(N.B. Most of these questions are self-explanatory, but I have put a few notes in to make the questionnaire a little more helpful.)

1. Describe the room, for example, is it bright, dark, warm, cold, open-plan, cluttered, cramped, spacious, noisy, calm, busy, etc.?

We all differ in our sensory needs and our personal space requirements. Some rooms are just too small for some people to feel comfortable in, others may be too large. If you can notice where a child seems to feel most secure, you may be able to structure the environment more supportively. Some people need more personal space between them and others; if a room is too small to allow this, behaviour can be adversely affected. Some people need more quiet than others. Check the noise levels and see if you feel they may be impacting on the child's learning and behaviour.

2. Sketch the room noting positions of doors, windows, teacher's desk, child's desk, light and dark areas, etc.

Where we are in relation to doors can create tension or ease. If you feel anxious you may not enjoy feeling penned in and far away from a door. Windows allow for distractions to enter your sensory realms, again adding to difficulties concentrating on tasks set. Children with attachment issues may feel much better if they are near to the teacher's desk. Some children feel happier sitting alone, others want to be close to others. All of these environmental aspects are worth looking at. Note down the layout of the room, then watch for behaviours, make slight changes and watch for changes in behaviour.

3. Note the predominant colour in the room.

Colour can have a big affect on mood.

4. What behaviours seem to cause concern?

5. Describe how the child 'does' this behaviour.

It's always a good idea to actually try to describe what the child is doing, sometimes we don't really describe very well. The very act of stopping and thinking about the behaviour can sometimes help us to understand why it is happening, and what we need to do to respond positively to it. Remember all behaviour is communication. Also if you can encourage the child to say how they 'do' certain behaviour, you have started the process of working out what doing something else will look like.

6. Have you noticed at what times of day and during which sessions/activities the behaviour seems to be more of a problem?

We all have times of the day when we are more lively and able to work than others. When we set tasks for children it is worth bearing this in mind.

---

7. Have you noticed any triggers for this behaviour?

Later in the book you will see the ABC model of observation described. A=antecedent, B=behaviour and C=consequences. This question just focuses on A, the antecedent or trigger for the behaviour causing problems.

---

8. How are other children involved in this behaviour?

---

9. What does the child get from behaving in this way?

Working out what the child is gaining from the behaviour may help in finding a substitute to fulfil the need the behaviour is fulfilling.

10. If the child didn't do this, what would he not get?

11. If this behaviour stopped, what would the child get?

12. What do other children get from this behaviour?

13. What would other children not get if this behaviour stopped?

14. If this behaviour stopped, what would the other children get?

15. What strategies have you tried that have been effective?

16. What have you changed in the environment that has been effective?

17. At which times does the child behave well?

18. Where is the child when this happens?

_____

19. Who is the child with when this happens?

_____

20. What is the activity the child is engaging with when this happens?

_____

21. Do you feel there are any other important factors about the child's learning environment that have not been mentioned here? If so, what are they and how do you feel they are important?

How to use this information

You now have lots of information about the environment within which the child finds him/herself when expected to learn. Part of the usefulness of the questionnaire is that it gets the person completing the form, unconsciously problem solving as they complete it. This information may reveal some simple spatial changes that could be made to improve things. You are also likely to want to do classroom observations and an ABC observation as outlined below to complement the information you have from above. Putting all of these pieces of information together will help to make an informed education plan.

Behavioural observation – time sampling

In your work as TA you may have carried out observations of children or seen advisory teachers and educational psychologists carry out observations. It is very likely that they have used a behavioural assessment that looks at the behaviour over a period of time in the classroom.

One criticism of behaviourism is its apparent focus on the problem rather than what we want to see, or the solution. A time-sampling sheet enables the observer to be objective in his/her observations as far as time is concerned. How often have you heard it said 'so and so *never* behaves himself'? My first question here would be 'Never?', as keeping up poor behaviour all of the time must be extremely hard work. My second is more concerned with semantics; 'behaves himself' – what does this really mean? We are behaving all of the time, in some shape or form. Through our behaviour we are communicating something. The interpretation of the behaviour is the important factor, and that is about a dynamic between the 'behaver' and the observer.

Time sampling then can give us some statistics on time spent behaving appropriately and inappropriately. Usually in a classroom observation we look for 'on-task' behaviour. This is generally indicated by the child being relatively sedentary, quiet, maybe talking a little relevant to the task, or engaging in 'good listening', i.e. sitting up straight and still, and looking at the speaker. Hopefully if these two conditions are fulfilled, thinking about what the speaker is saying, at the very least he/she will be acting as if he/she is listening. Understanding can be ascertained by asking questions. However, beware of disingenuous answers; it may just be that the communication style has not been tapped into sufficiently. Nonetheless classroom observations have their place, if only to convince teachers that their children are generally on-task, or to point to areas of practice that could do with some revamping to make lessons more accessible to children with a range of learning and communication styles.

I have found an observation sheet need only be a simple grid. Sampling can take place at intervals of two minutes or five minutes. At the point of observation the behaviour needs to be noted down, so for example, if a child is on-task, a tick can go in the box. You can, for extra information, as a footnote, note down what the child was doing to be on-task. Similarly, if the child is off-task, place a cross in the box, plus the number of the footnote and explain briefly the behaviour.

Opposite is an example from a couple of Joe's lessons. You met Joe earlier in the virtual group.

Name: Joe Bloggs   Age: 11

School: Reallygood City Technology College

Teacher: Nellie Jones   Subject: Critical thinking

Time of day: 1.30pm   Time interval: 2 minutes

								On	Off
X 1	X 1	✔ 2	✔ 2	✔ 3	✔ 3	✔ 3	✔ 3&4	6	2
X 5	X 6	X 7	X 8	X 9	X 10	✔ 11	✔ 11	2	6
✔ 11	✔ 12	✔ 12	✔ 13	✔ 13	✔ 14	break		6	0
							Totals	14	8
							%	64	36

1. head on desk – looked asleep
2. out of seat on-task
3. writing furiously
4. talking to neighbour
5. drawing/doodling
6. singing
7. swinging on chair
8. flicking Blue-tac
9. out of seat
10. disturbing others
11. doing 'special task' for Miss J – sorting a display
12. in seat listening to children read out their work
13. reading out his work
14. sitting up straight and still – good listening – to be chosen to go out to break.

Although a lively child, Joe was on-task for the majority of the lesson. However, the teacher did have to work hard to motivate him before he switched off, and ensure that there was something useful for him to do at the end of his period of hectic activity. He was keen to listen to others for a while, and very keen to read out his own work.

Look at another observation sheet of the same child with a different teacher a week later.

Name: Joe Bloggs   Age: 11
School: Reallygood City Technology College
Teacher: Betty Smith Subject: Critical thinking
Time of day: 1.30pm Time interval: 2 minutes

								On	Off
X 1	X 2	X 3	X 4	X 5	X 6	✔ 7	✔ 7	2	6
✔ 8	X 9	X 10	X 10	X 10	X 11	X 11	X 12	1	7
✔ 13	✔ 13	✔ 14	X 15	X 15	✔ 16	break		4	2
							Totals	7	15
							%	32	68

1. out of seat
2. sitting but talking to neighbour while teacher attempts to set up lesson
3. talking to neighbour on other side
4. shouting across room – should now be on-task – work has been set
5. out of seat attempting to get to child at other side of room – intercepted by teacher
6. arguing with teacher re validity of task – complaining it is boring

7. sitting close to teacher's desk doing work set
8. discussing task with teacher
9. teacher now moving around the room – Joe walks to rear of room to look out of window
10. out of room – toilet?
11. on re-entry to room he joins in with a group who are off-task
12. wandering round room – teacher catches up with him and redirects to seat close to her and to task
13. on-task, a bit fidgety, but compliant
14. presents task so far to teacher – for reassurance?
15. returns to seat, looking all around room dreamily
16. everything away – sitting up straight and still hoping to be picked to go out to play fast!!!

General observations:

Noisy room
Many children off-task
Teacher seemed to have poor grip of class
Task seemed uninteresting to many pupils

Clearly from this sheet we can see that the observation the previous week was, relatively speaking, a good one. This week the teacher finds it very hard to keep Joe on task. The task was a very reflective task that required quite a lot of writing to complete. The general feeling conveyed by the observation sheet is one of anxiety. Joe just did not seem settled, and did not seem to feel safe unless he was sitting close to the teacher. We see from the general observations that the noise level in the room was quite high, and that Joe was not alone in finding the task a bit troublesome. Joe showed his anxiety in a number of ways: he needed to be close to the teacher and he needed to go out of the room to the toilet. He possibly did genuinely need the loo, but that in itself could have been a nervous reaction to feelings of anxiety, or he could have been finding the work difficult so he felt the next best thing was to be out of the room completely – a way of getting a bit of a cooling off period. He was, in effect, self-regulating. This is a thing that as adults we do quite a lot – think about the number of times you feel you need a cup of tea or coffee (or a cigarette) – well that is self-regulation.

In your position as a TA, you will be able to make these observations and reflect on just what the behaviours of the child are telling you about what they need to feel calm enough to learn. Remember Maslow's hierarchy of needs discussed earlier in the book?

Activity

Complete an observation sheet of a child.

Name: School:

Teacher: Subject:

Time of day: Time interval:

								On	Off
							Totals		
							%		

Analysis of an observation sheet

A time sampling observation sheet can tell you all sorts of valuable information about a child and how he/she is finding the classroom situation. Human beings give out unconscious signals for other human beings to read in an attempt to get their needs met. Everyone does this. Neurologically most children are less well developed than most adults. Their needs may be wider ranging and less easily met. The theory of sensory integration put forward by Jean Ayres (1979) leads us to believe that children's sensory needs must be met to enable them to be in a comfortable state for learning. Going further back in time Maslow's (1954) hierarchy of needs also stated this. Children will tell us what they need. Sometimes they may need some deep muscle movement before they are able to switch on to learning. Think about yourself and the things that enable you to be more alert, and the things that calm you down, sometimes we need a piece of chocolate or a walk round the block, we are all different.

A time-sampling sheet is not worth doing unless you are going to analyse it and adapt the environment to help the child operate in it more successfully. To use it to try to prove a child is 'unteachable' is a travesty.

Activity

Complete an observation sheet of two children.

Now if you want to find out even more, take two children in one of the classes you work in. One child needs to have what you consider to be emotional and behavioural difficulties, the other should be a normally developing child.

Using the observation sheet above, complete for each of them under the same conditions – you should be able to do them both at the same time if you leave the time interval as long as 5 minutes. You can then compare the on- and off-task behaviour of both children. You may find it very interesting.

ABC model of observation

Another favourite of the behaviourists is the ABC of behaviour. A stands for antecedents, B for behaviour, and C for consequences.

Antecedents – events prior to the behaviour	Behaviour – as objective a description as possible	Consequences – events following the behaviour

You might like to think about an aspect of your own behaviour that is causing you some difficulty at the moment and do an ABC analysis. It could tell you what triggers your undesirable behaviour, and what the rewards for doing that behaviour are. When you have an idea of this you can think about the cost of giving up that behaviour. It may just be too much at the moment. Think then about a child you work with. Apply the same analysis. Can you understand why they don't want to change?

Doing these kind of exercises on yourself helps you to become better at empathizing with your students. To be good with children you need to know yourself.

Behaviour programmes

Frequently we try to help children change their behaviour by using some form of behaviour programme. A behaviour programme should be seen as a supportive tool to help the child keep focused on the appropriate desired behaviour. The big question here is who desires the behaviour? Too often children are told to change their behaviour without the reason for the behaviour – communication of the behaviour – being understood. Frequently adults around the child, unable to hold or contain the unwanted behaviour, want to eradicate it – to get rid of it, but without understanding what the behaviour is telling us we set ourselves up for later failure because, as the story at the beginning of this book indicates, the meaning will keep manifesting itself again and again in yet more and more inventive ways in an effort to be understood. It is always a good idea to try to find out what the behaviour is telling us, and to find out from the child which behaviours he/she thinks they want to change. It is possible that he/she has got stuck in patterns of behaviour that are no longer very useful to him/her and that, with a little external help, can be changed, but if the behaviour still has a function it will be hard to effectively shift, unless the communication is recognized. In the following section a method for constructing a behaviour programme with a child is explained. Later, methods for understanding the communication a child is trying to make will be explored.

My Success Book

Welcome to 'My Success Book'. The aim of 'My Success Book' is to have a conversation with the child which leads to the development of a behaviour plan. If you know a little bit about the child's interests (and hopefully you will because you will have built up rapport and been listening well), you can tailor the booklet to suit the child. In this case the child had a puppy called Kirby who modelled for the smiling and frowning dog pictures and the My Plan picture. If not, just use smiley faces or thumbs up instead.

You will see from 'My Success Book' that the objective is to enable the child to talk a little about him/herself, where he/she lives, who he/she lives with and what he/she is good at, before he/she moves on to thinking about the behaviours he/she exhibits that other people are not too keen on. He/she is then guided to think about the people these behaviours might be affecting, and most of all to think about the person who is most affected by the behaviour, i.e. him/herself, because he/she is the only person who is always with that behaviour. We are aiming for a 'buy in' here and a feeling that he/she owns the programme, not you, so the language used here needs to be very non-judgemental and the task of drawing out may take a lot of patience. The child needs to come to conclusions without you saying the words for him/her. It may take a few sessions to get to where you need to be before you start the programme. 'My Success Book' is as much about the non-judgemental relationship between you and the child as it is about the child making the effort to change. It is important for the same person to follow the process through with the child. The next task is to think about which of the behaviours would be the most easy to change and use that as the target. At this point it is imperative to ensure success, so the target needs to be achievable for the majority of the day. The next stage is to look together for a picture that the child likes. Trace the picture and split the day into 15-minute segments. This normally pans out at 25 in a day. Include breaks and lunchtime. As each 15-minute period goes by, a behaviour check is made and if the child is complying with the target, you initial the segment. If, for example, the requirement is to stay seated then, so long as he/she is seated at times when it is required, he/she gets the credit. If it is break or lunch he/she gets the credits free as there is no requirement to stay in your seat at that time so not to award the credit would penalize him/her unfairly. This way the child should pick up quite a few credits and start to feel that he/she actually does have some control over behaviour. If the child believes he/she can do it, there is a much greater chance that he/she will be able to do it, so our job is to give the child that confidence. Each day the child should be scoring between 15 and 20 credits. If not, the target is too hard to achieve and needs to be changed slightly. You will see from the picture of 'My Success Book' that an extra reward for good effort throughout the week is put in to help with training for longer term incentives – often an area of great difficulty. Also, the rewards are given as soon as 5, 10, 15, etc. segments are signed, NOT consecutively, but cumulatively. Remember whatever else the child has done that day, if he/she has complied with the target, he/she gets the reward. This programme focuses on one small target, one small step at a time, and is not dependent on good behaviour across the board. It is dependent on building in success for the child and helping him/her to recognize and savour what it feels like to get things right. The programme is deliberately hand drawn in conference with the child as it is the child's very own programme that no one else has had before.

My Success Book

 My name

 My address

 My school

 My teacher

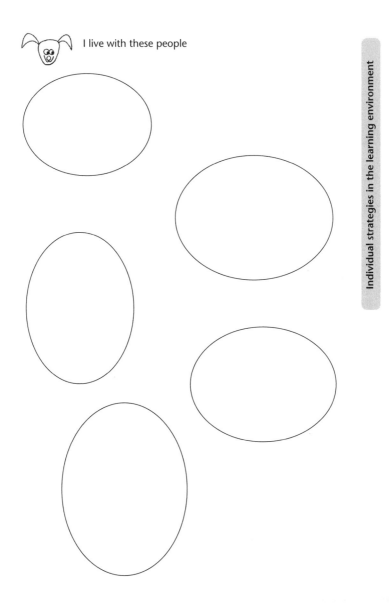

I live with these people

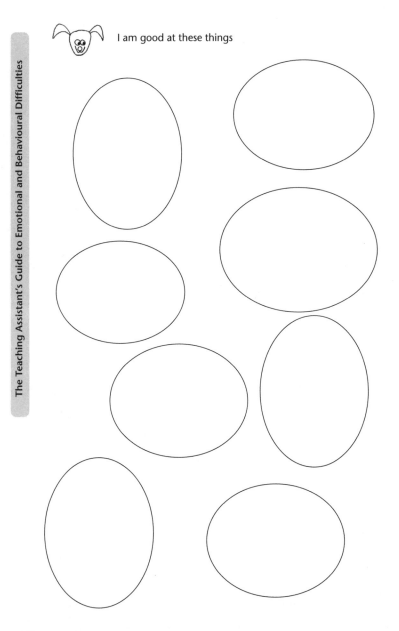

I am good at these things

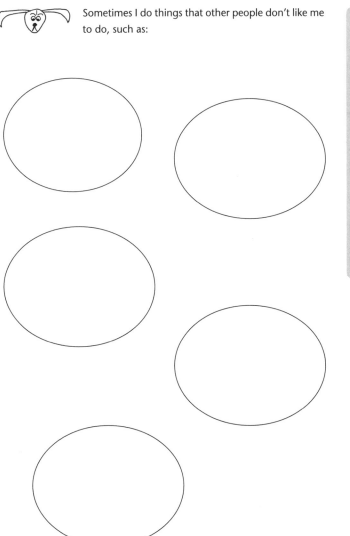

Sometimes I do things that other people don't like me to do, such as:

The people who get upset by these things are:

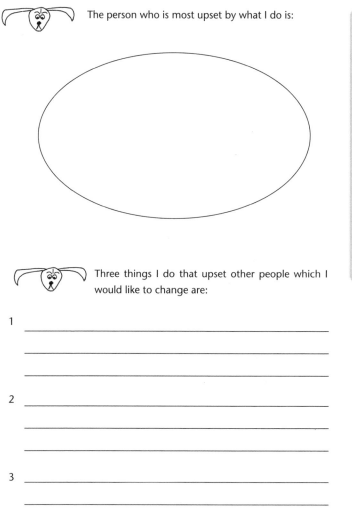

The person who is most upset by what I do is:

Three things I do that upset other people which I would like to change are:

1 _____

_____

_____

2 _____

_____

_____

3 _____

_____

_____

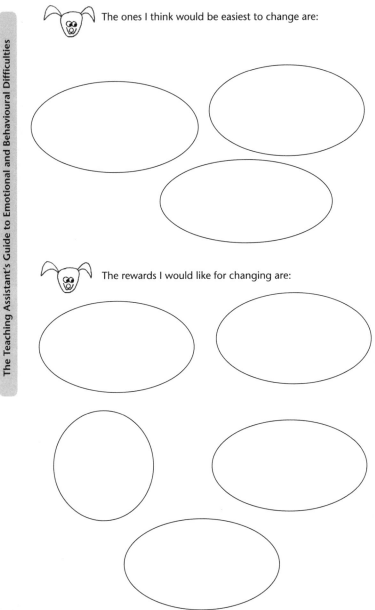

The ones I think would be easiest to change are:

The rewards I would like for changing are:

My Certificate of Success

Well done

_____

for changing your behaviour

Signed

_____

Class teacher

Signed

_____

Teaching Assistant

Signed

_____

Headteacher

Date _____

zone guided imagery

ided imagery below takes the young person through dif-
ime zones, starting with the unwanted behaviour in the
then gradually moving to the unwanted behaviour
thing of the past. It's amazing how useful the belief that
ed to do something, but no longer do, actually helps you
do that thing. Until your brain believes something it
reality for you.

re you start on this exercise it is useful to do a few relax-
xercises to get the young person in a receptive state.
an be quite simply done by asking the child to focus on
on the wall that is above eyelevel so that his/her head is
ightly tilted. Then suggest to him/her, keeping his/her
nd eyes still, to become aware of what is 20 cm either
the spot, now 30 cm, 50 cm, 1 metre, 3 metres, and all
d him/her. You are helping him/her to become aware of
in awareness of his/her peripheral vision. This is a great
for learning, in fact, for any change processes. Now,
t he/she thinks of the behaviour that is a problem. Really
, hear it and see it. Ask what the behaviour is? (Tell
er you are going to ask a few more questions, but you
want to hear the answers.)

re (*the behaviour*) ing.

ave this (*the behaviour*) ing.

ave been having a problem with (*the behaviour*).

ave that problem with (*the behaviour*).

sed to have that problem with (*the behaviour*).

ad what you need to change behaviour and in the past
ged to change your behaviour and move on.

Any behaviour programme will only work for a short period of time before it needs refreshing. Another method of incentivizing good behaviour is the response cost version. This can seem a bit negative at first but can work with some children very well. Here the child has a bank of tokens at the beginning of the day, or week for older children may be appropriate, which are forfeited for unwanted behaviour. This works well with children who find it difficult to work towards a goal, and who have a stronger sense of preserving what they already have than gaining something they do not yet have. Always try the positive method first.

Whenever you stop using a particular reward system make sure you keep up the behaviour specific praise.

Conversation for change for older children

The format of 'My Success Book' may serve you well for the primary years, but as children mature and are able to engage in more abstract thought you will want to move to a more mature method of working through problems. Below is a series of questions that can be used to help stimulate reflection and bring about change.

Assuming you know the young person and have spent some time building up a rapport with him/her, both you and the young person know there are difficulties regarding the young person's behaviour in certain contexts. The interview script below can be used to help the young person understand what the behaviour does for him/her, how they do the behaviour, and to move towards looking for alternative behaviours that could be useful.

Why are we here?
To begin with you are unlikely to get to the root of why you are there, so this question needs to be repeated a few times to get through the red herrings.

Why else?

If you don't get to the behaviours that are causing problems continue asking this question a few more times. It is **very very** important at this stage to have suspended judgement and to refrain from jumping in and answering the questions for the young person. Remember to listen with your eyes, ears, heart and undivided attention – remember the Chinese symbol for 'to listen'. There may be some silences lasting a few seconds which feel uncomfortable to begin with, but you would be surprised what problem solving can take place if you take the time to listen.

How do you know you have this problem with your behaviour?

This is where we ask for evidence that there is a problem. Check it out from another perspective.

What tells you that you have this problem?

This may be a chance for the young person to say that the feedback he/she gets from the teacher tells him/her that he/she has a problem with his/her behaviour. It may also reveal that he/she cannot see a problem, so there is no real ownership of the problem. This isn't a good time to start preaching and trying to put the perspective of everyone else. Keep listening and suspend judgement for now as you are learning and calibrating why the behaviour takes place, and what the benefit is to the young person.

How do you 'do' this problem?

This is where the young person has to think about what he/she looks like, feels like, sounds like etc., when he/she is doing this behaviour. When you know what you do, you can think of ways to do it differently. The saying 'if you always do what you have always done, you'll always get what you've always got' is worth remembering here. If someone wants to get different results in life, try different tactics.

How long have you had the probl
Was there a time when you didn't
This question helps the young pers
in actual fact he/she didn't have thi
behave in an acceptable way, when
and good self-esteem. It is of cour
not be able to remember such a tim
access this in the memory.

Once you have ascertained the un
start asking questions which help th
different way, for example try using

What wouldn't happen if you did (*t*

What isn't happening if you are (*the*

What would happen if you did (*the*

What is happening if you are (*the be*

What wouldn't happen if you didn't

What isn't happening if you're not (*t*

What would happen if you didn't (*th*

What happens if you don't (*the behav*

What is happening if you're not (*the b*

Time

The g
feren
preser
being
you u
to no
isn't a

Bef
ation
This
a spo
very
head
side
arou
being
state
sugg
feel
him/
don'

You

You

You

You

You

You
mar

You have felt resourceful and sometimes created new opportunities.

You have even been feeling resourceful.

As you are feeling resourceful saying this to yourself, now think about that problem you had and how much more resourceful you'll be feeling in the future, now.

See the problem behaviour, how has it changed?

Summary

This chapter has taken you through looking at the environment within which the child finds him/herself, looking directly at the behaviour of the child, and also looked at ways of communicating with primary and secondary age children with a view to helping them to change towards better behaviour patterns. Some of the techniques are NLP based. If you find them interesting and would like to know more, you might consider attending a course. NLP is very much about practice and 'getting it into the muscle'. Go to www.katespohrer.org.uk to find out about training for people in education.

Now that you have read through the different techniques and psychological perspectives you might like to look back at our 'Virtual EBD Group' and see if there are any techniques you would use with them. Throughout your reading you will unconsciously have been applying the ideas in the book, as well as many of your own that will have been flooding your mind, to pupils you work with.

Chapter 4 review

Quiz

		Yes	No	Maybe
1	Looking at the space within which a child is expected to operate can help in planning for better behaviour.	☐	☐	☐
2	Personal space requirements cannot be catered for in schools.	☐	☐	☐
3	All children feel happier sitting with other children.	☐	☐	☐
4	Looking at different pieces of information about a child is confusing and results in muddled IEPs.	☐	☐	☐
5	Time-sampling observation sheets are the best form of observational data you can get.	☐	☐	☐
6	A behaviour programme that is co-written with the child is more likely to be successful than one written for them.	☐	☐	☐
7	'My Success Book' involves the child at all stages of negotiations.	☐	☐	☐
8	Small achievable targets, one step at a time, are the key to success.	☐	☐	☐
9	Changing what we believe about our own behaviour changes our behaviour.	☐	☐	☐
10	Each teacher creates a different environment as does each room.	☐	☐	☐

	Yes	No	Maybe

11 Once rapport has been established with a young person you can use a 'conversation for change', sequence of questioning and 'time-zone guided imagery' to facilitate change.

12 Enabling a person to feel he/she has some control over his/her behaviour is a key to behavioural change.

13 The position of doors and windows in a classroom should make no difference to a child's behaviour.

14 Time sampling is a very useful tool because it often shows just how much a child is actually on-task rather than off it.

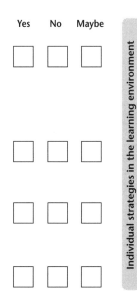

Individual strategies in the learning environment

5

Professional supervision in schools

Coping with your own emotions – keeping a journal

One of the biggest problems in coping with the challenge of EBD is that of looking after yourself so that you are able to give your best to situations and respond in an emotionally contained and containing way. Schools are unique to the helping professions in that they have no requirement for the kind of professional supervision that helps to support and maintain this ability. Any social worker coming into education will express amazement that this crucial aspect of mental health of the workforce is absent. One way to go some way towards helping to maintain your sanity is to keep a reflective journal. A journal of this nature allows you to candidly record your thoughts, feelings and reflections, and, importantly, illustrate to you that all things pass, even those situations that at the time seem unending and intolerable. Somehow too, the mere act of writing a journal helps you to think things through and get them into perspective.

A TA who had regularly completed the reflective journal had this to say about her experience:

> The reflective practice has made a big difference to the way I do my work. All of the time I am looking at the situation from the perspective of both insider and outsider. It's a bit like being a fly on the wall, you have to step outside of yourself and look at what you are doing. I can honestly say that I will always keep a professional journal from now on.

It's fascinating to look back at this time last year, or a few months ago and look at what was important at the time. It shows up just how much you forget. It also makes you consider your actions a lot more, and it makes you more confident about making decisions. Sometimes you forget the scary bits and the decisions you made. These all take their toll when you work with people, you have to take on so much emotionally that it's cathartic to be able to write it down, and even better when you can do some role reversal and really get into the skin of the person who is causing you angst. I know that this experience has made me a better practitioner and a stronger person.

Work discussion groups, the group mind and supervision

If you ever get the chance to attend a work discussion group, or reflective team you will find it very beneficial, supportive and professionally developmental. The reflective team method goes like this (DfES 2003, Cooke & Spohrer 2005): a staff member brings a work related problem to the group (or team). The facilitator will then interview the presenter who has 10–15 minutes to explain the problem to the group. The group members are then asked if they want any point clarified. At this point no problem solving takes place. The presenter then physically moves out of the group and silently observes the group discussing their problem. This is an extremely powerful device but requires the facilitator to be very firm in ensuring the presenter does not interfere with the free thinking of the group. At this point it is important to allow the group mind to go wherever it sees fit. This is where different ways of seeing a problem can emerge, and consequently different ways of solving it. After discussion of around 10–15 minutes the presenter is brought back into the group to comment on the discussion. If it was deemed appropriate by the facilitator, the psychodramatic technique of role reversal may be used to enable the presenter to feel a little more of what it is like to be in the shoes of the person with the problem, and thus enable more choices of action when next confronted with the situation under discussion. It can be a risky process, but feedback suggests it is exceedingly useful to listen, just listen, to others talking about your problem. This kind of reflective practice uses the group mind.

The facility afforded by psychodrama of 'role reversal' gives an individual a fantastic insight into how the person you are having the problem with is feeling. By being placed in his/her shoes, addressed by his/her name, and being required to answer questions as if you are that person, from your unconscious mind, is an extremely powerful experience. It is one of those experiences that can have a lasting impact and enables massive personal growth in a short space of time. These sessions always need to be run by a skilled facilitator.

One of the great benefits of attending a group comes from the building of a 'group mind'. The group mind is likely to see things in a different way to each of the individuals in the group. This can cause useful conflict, and will certainly provoke lively thinking. This is something that no matter how resourceful you are alone, you can never substitute for involving other minds in the problem solving process. The old saying 'a problem shared is a problem halved' is never truer than in this situation.

These are some comments from recent groups:

I have got so many new ideas from having this discussion.

The group sessions have definitely improved my classroom practice; I'm less likely to jump to the wrong conclusions now, more patient, more understanding of my problems and consequently the pupils' problems. It's really helped.

Helping schools develop new ways of working

Supervision, commonplace in other helping professions, is infrequently found in education. Introduction of reflective teams in schools empowers individuals to think more creatively about how to face problems in school with the emphasis shifting from one of within child towards environmental. Reflective practice encourages professional creativity. This in turn leads to increased job satisfaction due to a feeling of working with clients and creatively managing problems. It also encourages a move away from the dependency culture, to one of enabling and facilitating support in such a way that schools are encouraged to work collaboratively to address their problems – a systemic approach to problem solving. Everyone in a school can benefit from supervision of this sort. The comments below endorse this view:

> Doing role reversal in the psychodrama session gave me a fantastic insight into how the person I was having the problem with felt. I have never done anything like that before. It has made a lasting difference to the way I see things now. I wish all teachers had the chance of this. *A teacher*

> That was really useful. I have got a lot of things to think about, a lot of things I wouldn't have thought of myself. I would like more of our staff to come and see you and get this sort of help. *Deputy Head*

The comments below from a member of support staff who attended a supervision group indicate the positive nature of the work. The group was run by a teacher and an educational psychologist. The objective of the group was to provide support through a clinical supervision model and to pass on supervision skills to group members to enable them, over time, to become confident enough to co-work such groups themselves and to go on to further training in group supervision methods. Work discussion groups have been shown to have a significant impact on the thinking, attitudes and culture within a school (Jackson 2002).

We call it supervision and we joke about it, in a good way, as being counselling. It happens every fortnight, but I'd like it every week; I love it. There are usually seven of us, sometimes ten, and the facilitators who run the group. It enables us to talk about things that are bothering us. We describe a problem we are having and then get ten different thoughts on the problem. One of us describes the problem to the group, then sits away from the group and listens to their thoughts on what you have said. You can't talk at this point, but you can later into the group. Then you can comment on what the others have said. It was strange to begin with, and felt a bit weird not being able to talk at times, but after the first session we had learned the process; now we just do it. If it stopped, I would miss it. We've never had it before, it's very different from talking to your line manager – it's a totally different kind of supervision. It really helps to have other thoughts, not just your own thoughts governing a situation. It brings you closer to people. We did some psychodrama one week – that was weird. I had to imagine I was someone else, I got upset doing it, but I would do it again. It was good. It would be good for teachers too.

Benefits of multidisciplinary working

As a result of Every Child Matters all of us who work with children are being encouraged to work in an increasingly multidisciplinary way with health, social services, youth offending and many other agencies. Where this opportunity exists and is taken advantage of it can result in a much improved service for the child, and after all, the child should always be considered as our client, not the school or even the family. Multidisciplinary working has contributed to an increased ability to implement new ideas, and quicker and more efficient problem solving. Working together with other professions enables clearer pictures of processes that had previously been unclear and a greater understanding and tolerance of other professions and their role. Different professional groups all bring with them different aspects to each situation; these aspects are valuable and enable a fresh look at problems.

The increased understanding of how other agencies outside education think and approach problems enables work in schools to move away from the entrenched position that can endure when an organization persistently looks inwards for solutions. Sometimes thinking in this way is difficult and causes fear and resistance. You may have come across a bit of this yourself as a TA. TAs have a relatively new role in schools, and sometimes their ideas are looked on with great suspicion. Nonetheless you need to continue to 'think out of the box' and look at situations with the freshness your position gives you. In addition ensure as much as possible that you attend any multi-disciplinary meetings held about children you work with. The meetings are for problem solving, and should be a dynamic event where people think together and come up with ways forward, not simply report what they have or haven't been able to achieve since the last meeting. Your thoughts are needed at these meetings. Do not be afraid to speak up when you have something valuable to contribute.

Multidisciplinary working holds great opportunities for the future of children's welfare, but only if people pull together and put aside their professional jealousies.

Review

Because the nature of this chapter is quite personal and reflective I have not included a quiz. I hope that you will think for a while about what you have read, and that you may even decide to put pen to paper and start your own professional journal, or look out for a work discussion group near you. If you would like help setting one up in your school send an email to me at kate@katespohrer.co.uk. I hope you have enjoyed reading this book and found it useful to your practice. If you have any questions please contact me at the email address above.

Useful websites

www.crisisprevention.co.uk

www.toddlertime.com/advocacy/pat/person-feelings.htm

www.katespohrer.org.uk

www.youngminds.org.uk

www.sebda.org

www.nasen.org.uk

References

Ainsworth, M. D. S., Blehar, M. C., Waters, E. and Wall, S. (1978), *Patterns of Attachment: A Psychological Study of the Strange Situation.* Hillsdale, NJ: Erlbaum.

Arnold, C. and Yeomans, J. (2005), *Psychology for Teaching Assistants.* Stoke on Trent: Trentham Books.

Ayres, A. J. (1979), *Sensory Integration and the Child.* Los Angeles, CA: Western Psychological Services.

Ayers, H., Clarke, D. and Murray, A. (2000), *Perspectives on Behaviour.* London: David Fulton Publishers.

Bion, W. (1967), *Second Thoughts.* London: Karnak.

Bennathan, M. and Boxall, M. (2000), *Effective Intervention in Primary Schools: Nurture Groups* (2nd edn). London: David Fulton.

Bowlby, J. (1982), *Attachment and Loss. Vol. 1: Attachment* (2nd Edn). New York: Basic Books (new printing, 1999, with a foreword by Allan N. Schore; originally published in 1969).

Chopra, D. (1989), *Quantum Healing.* New York: Bantam New Age Books.

Cooper, P. and Tiknaz, Y. (2007), *Nurture Groups in School and at Home.* London: Jessica Kingsley Publishers.

Spohrer, K. and Cooke, C. (2005), 'A problem shared'. *Special Children*, 166, 27–29.

DfES (2001), *The Revised SEN Code of Practice.* London: DFES.

DfES (2003), *Development Programme for Behaviour and Education Support Teams – Handbook.* London: DfES.

DfES (2003), *Good Practice Guidance for Behaviour and Education Support Teams*. London: DfES.

Gardner, H. (1993), *Multiple Intelligences*. New York: Basic Books.

Grinder, J. and Bandler, R. (1989), *The Structure of Magic: A Book About Language and Therapy v. 1 (Structure of Magic)*. Palo Alto, CA: Science and Behavior Books.

Goleman, D. (1996), *Emotional Intelligence*. London: Bloomsbury.

Jackson, E. (2002), 'Mental health in schools: what about the staff?'. *Journal of Child Psychotherapy* 28: 2, 129–146.

Kelly, G. (1955), *The Psychology of Personal Constructs*, Vol. I.II. New York: Norton.

Maslow, A. (1954, reprinted 1970), *Motivation and Personality*. New York: Harper & Row.

Appendix

Chapter 1 review – Quiz

	Yes	No	Maybe

1 The humanistic approach to understanding EBD emphasizes meeting people's basic needs. ✓

2 Abraham Maslow created a hierarchy of needs believing basic needs should be met before higher order things can be considered. ✓

3 All behaviour is a kind of communication. Training in Neuro-Linguistic Programming enables the practitioner to calibrate behaviour and read unconscious signals. ✓

4 Humanistic psychology believes in setting up to succeed by meeting needs and enabling a person to do well. ✓

5 Behaviouristic psychology is concerned with a person's inner feelings rather than outward expressions. (No ✓)
Behaviouristic psychology is concerned with outward manifestations rather than what is going on inside.

	Yes	No	Maybe

6 Behaviourism believes genetics has a big role to play in determining how we behave.
Behaviouristic psychology largely denies genetic influence.

7 To be successful with people with behaviour difficulties, we need to keep reflecting on our own behaviour as well as other people's.

8 Behaviourism is concerned with our unconscious processes.

9 Behaviourism concentrates on training.

10 Cognitive behavioural psychology appreciates different people respond in different ways to stimuli and grew out of the behaviourist school of psychology.

11 The psychodynamic approach believes the origin of behavioural difficulties stems from the unconscious mind.
Early experiences affect unconscious processes.

12 Attachment theory was born out of behaviouristic thinking.
Attachment theory grew out of the psychodynamic school of thought.

	Yes	No	Maybe

13 Difficult behaviour is often directed at someone rather than the cause of the problem.

14 Social learning theory developed from the behaviourist school and focuses on modelling.

15 Ecosystemic theory looks at isolated acts.
Ecosystemic theory looks at the behaviour as part of a system rather than as isolated acts.

16 Biological theory attributes much behaviour to genetic components.

17 The constructivist approach believes we all operate like scientists, testing hypotheses as we go through life and changing according to the results we find.

18 EBD covers a narrow range of issues all to do with acting out behaviour.
EBD covers a wide range of behaviour including 'acting in' or very withdrawn behaviour as well as the more obvious 'acting out' behaviour.

19 One of the greatest gifts for coping with difficult behaviour is a good sense of humour and the ability to laugh at yourself.

Chapter 2 review – Quiz

	Yes	No	Maybe

1 A nurture group consists of one teacher and three children.
   Nurture groups vary, but will commonly be for no more than ten children and always have two adults.

2 Preparing and eating food together with two supportive adults who are modelling the role of good parents is part of the daily nurture group activity.

3 Children are not allowed to choose what and how they want to play in a nurture group.
   The opportunity to choose activities is an essential part of the nurture group experience.

4 Rapport is something you either have or you don't – you cannot learn how to do it.
   Rapport can easily be learned by practising the exercises in this book.

5 Nurture groups are always run in nurseries.
   Nurture groups are more often run in primary schools than secondary, but some enlightened secondary schools are running nurture groups.

	Yes	No	Maybe
6 Nurture groups are not appropriate for children of secondary school age.	☐	✓	☐
7 Training in Neuro-Linguistic Programming enables you to tune in to people's unconscious signals and so understand them better.	✓	☐	☐
8 In NLP we understand that everyone has their own version of reality and that we need to accept it will be different from ours.	✓	☐	☐
9 Mirroring people helps build rapport.	✓	☐	☐
10 Attachment theory was first suggested by John Bowlby.	✓	☐	☐
11 Children resent secure boundaries. *Children need secure boundaries, as do adults.*	☐	✓	☐
12 A child rejected by his/her mother may exhibit avoidant attachment patterns.	✓	☐	☐
13 Finding out a person's representational system and translating from your system to another person's will help build trust and communication.	✓	☐	☐
14 Good schools provide emotional containment for their staff and pupils.	✓	☐	☐

Chapter 3 Review – Quiz

	Yes	No	Maybe

1   Discipline problems usually arise from anxiety because physiological, safety and belonging needs are not being met.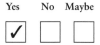

2   It is better not to allow the feelings of a child affect how you feel in a situation. *You need to register the feelings you get from the child and acknowledge that they will be feeling that way too and are transferring their feelings to you. You can use your feelings as an emotional barometer for the child.*

3   Abraham Maslow believed children can learn without having their safety needs met.

4   You can always predict difficult situations arising. *If you calibrate a person's behaviour it is very rare that you will not be able to predict behaviour, but you do have to become skilled and keep vigilant.*

5   Rapport can be used to good effect to gain information about a person's behaviour

6   Being an assertive communicator means you always end up getting your way. *Assertive communication is about compromise and negotiation.*

	Yes	No	Maybe

7 Children can learn assertive communication styles from adults in school. *Modelling good coping methods of communication helps children to learn how to cope with situations.*

8 Listening requires periods of silence. *Winston Churchill is reputed to have said, 'Courage is what it takes to stand up and speak; courage is also what it takes to sit down and listen.' We need to pay particular attention to keeping quiet for long enough to allow people to feel they have been listened to, and for us actually to have listened to them.*

9 The broken record technique is a passive way of communicating. *Broken record is an assertive way to communicate and very effective once you have got used to using it.*

10 Using positive self talk is a great way to boost confidence to do things we feel unsure about.

Chapter 4 Review – Quiz

1 Looking at the space within which a child is expected to operate can help in planning for better behaviour.

		Yes	No	Maybe

2 Personal space requirements cannot be catered for in schools.
Personal space requirements must be catered for in schools. Ignore at your peril.

3 All children feel happier sitting with other children.

4 Looking at different pieces of information about a child is confusing and results in muddled IEPs.
For best results triangulate different sources of data.

5 Time-sampling observation sheets are the best form of observational data you can get.
All data is useful, but no one piece or perspective should be relied on exclusively.

6 A behaviour programme that is co-written with the child is more likely to be successful than one written for him/her.

7 'My Success Book' involves the child at all stages of negotiations.

8 Small achievable targets, one step at a time, are the key to success.

	Yes	No	Maybe

9 Changing what we believe about our own behaviour changes our behaviour. ✓

10 Each teacher creates a different environment as does each room. ✓

11 Once rapport has been established with a young person you can use a 'conversation for change' sequence of questioning and a 'time-zone guided imagery' to facilitate change. ✓

12 Enabling a person to feel he/she has some control over his/her behaviour is a key to behavioural change. ✓

13 The position of doors and windows in a classroom should make no difference to a child's behaviour. ✓ (No)
Positions of distractions can make a big difference to success in a class-room.

14 Time sampling is a very useful tool because it often shows just how much a child is actually on-task rather than off it. ✓
This evidence can be used to reframe the child from being one always off-task to one who needs a few environ-mental changes to function better. It can also show just what activities the child feels able to engage with so is a springboard for further action.

Assertiveness styles table – completed example.

What do you do when you do . . .	. . . assertive	. . . aggressive	. . . passive/ aggressive	. . . passive
	Honest and open. Actively listens to another viewpoint. Empathizes with the situation of other people. Clear, well thought through argument. Ability to achieve a compromise and workable solution. Express your point of view clearly but with regard for the feelings of others.	Get your own way no matter what. Push your own point across. Coerce people into doing things they don't feel comfortable doing. Violent or loud behaviour. Interrupt others.	Refuse to engage by remaining silent. Agree to suggestions but quietly do nothing about them. Sit back when things need to be done.	Remain silent in fear of upsetting others. Avoid confrontation. Say 'yes' when you mean 'no'. Puts other people's wishes before your own needs. Bottle up feelings and remain quiet. Apologise for your actions when not necessary.

What don't you do when you do . . .	. . . *assertive*	. . . *aggressive*	. . . *passive/ aggressive*	. . . *passive*
	Belittle others. Push your point across at all costs. Rush to conclusions. Score points. Make people feel uneasy deliberately.	Encourage others to have their say. Actively listen to the point of view of someone else. Allow time for thinking and discussion. De-escalate difficult situations.	Communicate feelings and thoughts verbally.	State your view when you feel it necessary in a coherent manner.

What are the non-verbal clues when you are . . .	. . . assertive	. . . aggressive	. . . passive/ aggressive	. . . passive
	Stand in a supportive manner, shoulders and body at an oblique angle. When gesticulating, keeping palms upwards communicating openness to the ideas of others. Match and mirror actions of the other person. Breathing calmly.	Square up in confrontational style. Clenched fists. Breathing may be quick. Finger drumming.	Remain silent. May look as if being compliant.	Down-trodden look. Shoulders droop. Darting or downcast eyes. Nervous tics. Hand wringing.

What are the verbal clues when you are . . .	. . . assertive	. . . aggressive	. . . passive/ aggressive	. . . passive
	Voice controlled and clear. Match and mirror tone and volume. Listen – leave time for the other person to talk.	Racing speech. Raised voice. Basic vocabulary. May be some swearing/ slang.		Hesitancy. Quiet voice or no voice. Says 'yes' to everything.

Appendix